Breaking New Ground:
Teaching Students with Limited
or Interrupted Formal Education
in U.S. Secondary Schools

Andrea DeCapua

The College of New Rochelle

and

Helaine W. Marshall

Long Island University

Ann Arbor
University of Michigan Press

Published in the United States of America
The University of Michigan Press
Manufactured in the United States of America

♾Printed on acid-free paper

ISBN-13: 978-0-472-03452-9

2014   2013   2012   2011   4   3   2   1

Acknowledgments

WE WISH TO THANK the following colleagues, students, friends, and family members who have been instrumental in helping us with this book. Diana Berkowitz, Mary Carpenter, Alice Dunning, Iris Goldberg, Judith Hausman, Andrea Honigsfeld, Ann Hoskins, Joanna Labov, Nancy Lemberger, Patricia McMahon, Ingrid Merli, Rebecca Rich, and Sidonie Schneider all read portions of the manuscript and provided valuable feedback. We especially appreciate the contribution of Hugh Marshall, who read the entire manuscript for clarity and consistency. Carol Antolini, Betty Cicero, Janice Galt, Renee Finneran, Ann Marie Keinz, Rosa Peña, Erika Perez, Madeleine Reyes, and Gloria Rodriguez were among the teachers who graciously let us into their classrooms. Nicole Nyguen and Son Pham are two of the many students who willingly shared their work with us. Hope Herzog was our able and conscientious graduate assistant who assisted us with the paperwork.

We would also like to thank our respective institutions, The College of New Rochelle and the Westchester Graduate Campus of Long Island University, for their support.

Contents

Introduction

We never had a lot of students who couldn't speak English in our school district until the last couple of years. And a lot of these ESL students have hardly been in school at all, even though they're teenagers.

—ESL teacher, Iowa

U.S. SCHOOLS ARE ENROLLING EVER LARGER NUMBERS of children who speak a first language other than English and who are English language learners (ELLs). The number of ELLs in Grades K–12 more than doubled in the 16 years between the 1989–1990 school year and the 2005–2006 school year. ELL enrollment increased nearly seven times the rate of total K–12 student enrollment (National Clearinghouse for English Language Acquisition, 2008).

Many of these ELLs have had little or no experience with formal education or their education has been interrupted for extended periods of time. Exact data in terms of how many ELLs have limited, interrupted, or no formal education are difficult to obtain given ambiguities in determining exactly who falls into this category. Many schools, for example, do not separate this subpopulation of ELLs from their other ELLs in their data collection (Short, 2002). In addition, there have been differences in how this subgroup of ELLs is identified and described. It is not always easy to distinguish SLIFE from other ELLs initially. While it is straightforward to identify those who enter high school with no or very limited schooling and native language literacy, a wide range exists in the abilities of other ELLs who may or may not be part of this subpopulation of ELLs. ELLs who previously attended a U.S. school and then returned home before returning again to continue their education in the U.S., for example, may or may not fall into this category, depending on whether their schooling was interrupted or continued when they returned home.

Many factors contribute to the limited or interrupted educational experiences of this subpopulation of ELLs. Their education may have been interrupted because of war, civil conflict, migration, or economic necessities requiring them to work or care for younger family members. Others may come from countries with low literacy rates, where only a minority has learned to read and write in their native language. Even those who come from countries with substantial literacy levels, such as China, may not have been able to participate fully in the educational system (Rong & Shi, 2001). Access to education in many countries is limited, especially in rural areas, and often such schooling is available only for early elementary grades. When adequate school-

1

ing is available, there may be few public schools and education may be costly, requiring the purchase of school uniforms, textbooks, and other materials. Education may be further limited due to the inadequate preparation of teachers, students' lack of familiarity with the language of instruction, and/or the prevalence of traditional pedagogical methods focusing primarily or exclusively on rote learning and memorization. For some or all of these reasons, schools may have been able to provide students with only the most rudimentary instruction (Gallegos, 2005; Guzmán, 2000). These and many other issues may hinder a quick and easy identification of these ELLs. A more in-depth discussion of determining which ELLs fit this profile is, however, beyond the scope of this book. We refer readers interested in this question to *Meeting the Needs of Students with Limited or Interrupted Schooling* (DeCapua, Smathers, & Tang, 2009).

Because formal education is so closely tied to literacy, ELLs who comprise this subpopulation high school commonly have literacy skills far below grade level, and may even be completely new to literacy. Although it is possible to become literate outside of the formal educational setting (Scribner & Cole, 1981), the students we have encountered generally enter the school system with little or no native language literacy. In addition to this major defining characteristic, it is important to note that they are a subgroup of ELLs and, therefore, do not speak English as a native language. Although it is true that students with limited or interrupted education can come from countries where English is spoken or from ethnic groups that speak English, the focus here will be on those for whom English is a new language, the great majority of SLIFE.

In the search for an appropriate term to use in referring to this subpopulation of ELLs, educators and researchers have used such labels as "Students with Interrupted Formal Education or SIFE" (New York State Department of Education), students with limited formal schooling, (e.g. Freeman & Freeman, 2002; Walsh, 1999), "newcomers" (e.g. Constantino & Lavadenz, 1993; Short, 2002), or "unschooled migrant youth" (e.g. Morse, 1997). In this book, we have adopted the acronym SLIFE—Students with Limited or Interrupted Formal Education, first used by DeCapua, Smathers, & Tang (2009) to refer to this subpopulation of ELLs. As reflected in these labels, regardless of ethnicity, country of origin, or native language, all these students enter the school system, often at the secondary level, with little or no exposure to formal education, which may or may not have been interrupted. At the secondary level, SLIFE are among those at the highest risk of dropping out (Fry, 2005). Note: Throughout this book, SLIFE (because *students* is plural) will appear as a plural and take a plural verb.

In addition to lacking proficiency in English and literacy skills, these students lack grade-level content knowledge, and, due to their limited exposure to schooling, frequently lack foundational content knowledge. Equally important, SLIFE frequently hold cultural values, beliefs, and assumptions that are often at odds with those of mainstream U.S. education.

SLIFE face cultural dissonance every day in the classroom, the hallways, the school grounds, and in all aspects of their school experience. We believe that before any program for SLIFE can be completely successful, it needs to address this underlying issue. In its most concrete terms, this can be seen in the comments from this teacher who details her early experiences with this population in her high school:

> *If you take this paper, even with the holes on the left side and the lines, they don't know what's the front, what's the back. They don't even know where to put their name and where to put the date. Sometimes they write their name right next to the date and maybe another time somewhere else. And their name could be anywhere. All their papers are all over. Even when I give them a binder and the tabs and dividers and sit down with them, it takes a long time and some of them don't get it for the longest time. They don't know what to do with the paper, even when I stay after school and help them organize.*

> —Janice, high school teacher of SLIFE, New York

Janice's comments highlight how unfamiliar even the basics of school are for SLIFE. While it is tempting to focus solely on such immediate and obvious needs of SLIFE, we must keep in mind that these represent the most readily apparent issues, and lie on the surface of what constitutes a much deeper problem. Many SLIFE are at risk for failure due to the vast differences between their expectations and the realities of how and what they are being taught (Gunderson, 2000). While we do not deny that high school SLIFE drop out for many reasons, often economic and/or family related, we also firmly believe that there is another significant factor that is not being sufficiently addressed in classes and programs for this population—cultural dissonance. Often teachers and administrators themselves are unaware of the complex, and often hidden, formal schemata that constitute the expected learning paradigm of Western-style education as it plays out in U.S. high schools today (Ladson-Billings, 1995; DeCapua & Marshall, 2010b). It is this hidden agenda of assumptions about learning, more than surface issues apparent in tasks such as creating and keeping a notebook, that is responsible for contributing to the feelings of alienation that SLIFE face each day in U.S. schools.

Cultural Assumptions

To illustrate the extent of this cultural dissonance, the major assumptions of main-stream U.S. teachers and students are summarized:

Assumptions of Teachers and Learners

1. The goals of K–12 instruction are
  a. to prepare the learner for life after schooling
  b. to produce an independent learner
2. The learner brings along
  a. an urge to compete and excel as an individual
  b. age-appropriate preparation for
    ▪ literacy development
    ▪ academic tasks

Adapted from Marshall, 1998; DeCapua & Marshall, 2010a, 2010b; Marshall, DeCapua, & Antolini, 2010.

Throughout this book, we explore how, from the perspective of SLIFE, these assumptions about teaching and learning are, for the most part, not valid. One by one, we address the issues and consequent cultural incongruity SLIFE face when confronted by an educational system based on these assumptions. We argue that because SLIFE come from a very different cultural orientation to learning, it is important not to view them as failing based on the assumptions of the U.S. system.

A New Instructional Model— The Mutually Adaptive Learning Paradigm

Reaching SLIFE entails not only addressing language and content, but also addressing culture. To minimize the sense of alienation SLIFE experience when entering U.S. schools and the concomitant negative effects on academic achievement, teaching must go beyond a compendium of best practices. Instruction for SLIFE also needs to go beyond culturally responsive pedagogy because focusing on providing culturally relevant materials is not enough (Gordon & Yowell, 1999).

In this book, we present a new instructional model, the Mutually Adaptive Learning Paradigm (MALP). This model provides teachers with a framework for understanding what will work and why (DeCapua & Marshall, 2010a, 2010b; Marshall & DeCapua, 2010; Marshall, DeCapua, & Antolini, 2010). SLIFE and U.S. educators hold, for the most part, very different assumptions about teaching and learning. The instructional model, MALP, makes these different assumptions explicit. Because MALP is mutually adaptive, the instructional model asks that both parties, SLIFE and

U.S. educators, recognize the critical priorities of the other so that SLIFE can transition to the practices and expectations of the U.S. educational system.

A note of caution about the SLIFE population is needed here. SLIFE are by no means a homogeneous group; they come from all over the world, from diverse languages, backgrounds, and life experiences, and we must be careful not to overgeneralize or stereotype these students when they enter our classrooms. Some SLIFE may have good colloquial or conversational English proficiency; some may have relatively strong literacy skills but have large gaps in content-area knowledge; still others may be entering school for the first time. We encourage teachers to see them as individuals in their classrooms and treat them as separate and different from each other, as for any other students they may have. We view them as a group so as to provide classroom teachers with guidelines. Regardless of their differences, these students, by virtue of having had limited, interrupted, or in some cases, no formal education, have a very different learning paradigm from that of mainstream U.S. schools and face cultural dissonance.

Steps Toward Implementation

What follows is a step-by-step overview of what teachers need to do before implementing this new instructional model, MALP, at the secondary level. Although MALP can be implemented at any grade level, we focus here on SLIFE at the secondary level since these are the students at highest risk of dropping out (Fry, 2005).

Step One: Administrative Approval

As for any new model of instructional delivery, teachers should obtain approval from a district-wide or building administrator before proceeding. Users of this book will have sufficient information and understanding of the model to make the case to their administrators and to respond to concerns that may arise. To have the school administration support efforts to implement MALP avoids feelings of isolation that teachers of SLIFE and these students often experience. Even if the class for SLIFE is the only place in the school where this model is implemented, such support allows teachers to adjust the grade-level curriculum, the pedagogical tools, the cultural climate, and other aspects of instructional delivery.

Step Two: Curriculum and Standards

In order to focus on appropriate content, teachers need to review the national, state and/or district standards. Because SLIFE will have significant gaps in their content-area knowledge and literacy abilities, teachers will want to look at the standards for previous grade levels, going back to the elementary grades, and use a combination of elementary and secondary level standards to create objectives for their lessons. This is not remediation, however, because SLIFE have not yet been exposed to the content-area knowledge and literacy practices expected of secondary students. The curriculum in classes for SLIFE needs to align with their actual current level of knowledge and skills. The intent of this book is to guide teachers' pedagogy; teachers are referred to resources already available to develop SLIFE curriculum (e.g., DeCapua, Smathers, & Tang, 2009; Echevarria, Vogt, & Short, 2008; Freeman & Freeman, 2002).

Step Three: Lesson Planning and Preparation

In planning to implement the model, teachers will view their lesson plans through the lens of MALP. Using MALP in preparing lessons requires teacher to revisit the assumptions outlined on the box on page 4 in a manner consistent with this model. First, teachers select the relevant standards and set daily objectives; then they guide the students toward completing class projects. Chapter 4 discusses writing lesson objectives targeted specifically for SLIFE in the context of MALP, and Chapter 5 outlines the principles of project-based learning using MALP.

Step Four: Applying the Instructional Model

This last step asks teachers to check that they are truly implementing MALP. Taking the lesson plans they have developed, teachers use the tools provided in this text to incorporate all the elements of the MALP instructional model. Teachers will find that they already address some elements in their lesson plans; at the same time they will find that other elements require altering their lessons. The MALP Checklist presented in Chapter 4 guides teachers in assessing how comprehensively they are applying the model into their lessons.

Considerations in Implementing MALP

Mixed Ability Classes

Before we embark on our exploration of the MALP instructional model and its foundations, we turn to issues that may arise as teachers of SLIFE begin to implement MALP.

Ideally, once such students have been identified, schools set up a self-contained program for SLIFE, addressing the needs of SLIFE in a separate program and separate classes. Schools with large numbers of SLIFE can and should take this approach. However, many schools lack sufficient numbers of such students. In such cases, SLIFE are typically mixed in with beginner ELLs, and implementing the MALP instructional model introduced in this text is a viable and advantageous solution. This model encourages success for all ELLs because it accepts cultural differences while promoting transitions to U.S. classrooms. Moreover, project-based learning, as outlined in this text, encourages and supports consistent and real differentiation of learning, and true cooperative learning is the norm. For the work in groups and in pairs, beginner ELLs with more formal education experience can act as "buddies," or peer mentors, for SLIFE (DeCapua, Smathers, & Tang, 2009). In so doing, these students practice and rehearse their own knowledge and further refine their academic English as they help their classmates. Care, of course, must be taken that these other ELLs are utilized in such a way that they, too, are developing and improving their knowledge and skills and not merely substituting as informal aides or teachers' helpers.

Covering the Curriculum

Public high school teachers have a mandated curriculum with both scope and sequence specified, and they are expected to keep to a schedule of unit completion that is based on the school calendar. While this may make it appear that incorporating the MALP instructional model could be problematic, or even contraindicated, we believe the opposite is the case. Strict adherence to a curriculum designed for students who are not SLIFE will not help them. If they are having difficulty with material, then pushing ahead to cover even more new material in the mandated curriculum is counterproductive. In lessons infused with MALP, on the other hand, learning is constantly scaffolded, and information is recycled and applied in a variety of ways to maximize opportunities for SLIFE to understand and internalize it.

An insistence on covering curriculum without attending to the needs of SLIFE means that these students will at best get a cursory or superficial understanding of the material. They can easily become bored, anxious, and frustrated and drop out (Freeman & Freeman, 2002). SLIFE need to be able to process information so that it becomes meaningful, which calls for a different approach to instruction. In our work, we have found that successful implementation of MALP shows promising results in motivating SLIFE and encouraging them to engage in school learning (DeCapua & Marshall, 2010b; Marshall, 1998; Marshall, DeCapua, & Antolini, 2010).

High-Stakes Testing and SLIFE

One of the most pressing problems teachers of SLIFE face is the requirement that all students must be tested using standardized assessments that are mandated at state and federal levels. This testing does not exclude SLIFE, even though they have little or no prior experience with school. Applying MALP in the classroom can both minimize the difficulties SLIFE face with respect to these assessments and assist teachers in creating a supportive testing environment for them.

The focus on standardized test scores as evidence of learning has required all teachers to place greater emphasis on preparing students to do well on the tests. Assessment is one of the greatest school challenges for SLIFE. In the U.S. educational system, regardless of the ongoing classroom activities that may take place, academic success hinges on testing. The testing situation almost always consists of a single student providing answers on a printed teacher-made or standardized assessment. There is, at the present time, no widely accepted or institutionalized alternative to this "bottom line." Although alternative assessments, such as portfolios, have been promoted, the challenge of testing has become even greater under current federal education policy. Schools that receive federal funding are required by law to demonstrate that their ELLs are making progress in developing English language proficiency via standardized assessments (U.S. Department of Education, 2007).

Furthermore, ELLs, like all other students in U.S. schools, are required to take grade-level content area knowledge tests in English, including English Language Arts, regardless of whether or not they have the language proficiency to do so. As Menken (2008) points out

> English language learners are now showered with tests from the moment they enter school . . . an immediate effect of [this] testing policy is that ELLS are overwhelmingly failing the tests, labeled as deficient and low-performing, and barred from advancement. (p. 35)

Menken and others (e.g., Abdei, Hofstetter, & Lord, 2004; Solano-Flores & Trumball, 2003) argue that, along with issues of English language proficiency, there are also cultural issues in these standardized tests that are designed for native speakers. Tests often include questions with subtle nuances of meaning that rely on a sophisticated knowledge of the language used in the question prompts. In addition, the test format is frequently an unfamiliar one that causes students to become disoriented. Menken found that many ELLs drop out after numerous failed attempts to pass required state and local assessments that consist largely of multiple choice and similar formats. She noted in particular that it was not primarily the content of the tests, but the language and the way the questions were posed that contributed to their lack of success. Others have reported that even advanced non-native speakers at the university level have difficulty with typical U.S. formal assessments (Bifuh-Ambe, 2009; Ibarra, 2001). The multiple choice format, for example, which is a common type of standardized assessment in the U.S., is not universally used in educational systems around the world, even those with Western-style schooling (Pinkus, 2009).

MALP transitions SLIFE to the type of thinking needed on standardized assessments rather than approaching high stakes testing from the test preparation perspective. SLIFE are generally not accustomed to tasks that ask them to make judgments but are looking instead for practice. SLIFE who have had some schooling prior to immigrating to the U.S. primarily experienced rote learning (Gallegos, 2005; Townsend & Fu, 2001). *What* they need to learn is emphasized rather than *how* to learn.

Based on our work with SLIFE and our instructional model, we support the argument that the tests themselves are assessing specific formal schemata that are not meaningful, relevant, or familiar to many SLIFE, even when they have been exposed to test-taking strategies designed to help them succeed on them. If we carefully examine the formats of these tests and realize that doing well on them is not simply a matter of a skill set, but a paradigm shift as well, we can perhaps begin to bring SLIFE to a place where they can shift their thinking.

Why This Book?

We endeavor in this book to elucidate an instructional model that provides a framework for classroom teaching, placing equal weight on language, content, and culture. Understanding the larger cultural issues is not a question of changing all our instructional approaches to meet the expectations and needs of SLIFE because this will not serve them well as they compete with their peers academically. What is needed is a mutually adaptive approach that includes language and content, while incorporating the cultural needs of SLIFE.

Breaking New Ground builds on the earlier book by DeCapua, Smathers, & Tang (2009), *Meeting the Needs of Students with Limited or Interrupted Schooling,* an introduction to this population. *Breaking New Ground* introduces readers to and engages them in the implementation of an instructional model that we have developed over many years of working with SLIFE. Although we do not intend to negate the value and importance of the researched-based best practices for these students, we believe that what is most sorely needed is a larger framework within which to place these practices. Central to the instructional model and the practices presented in this book is our belief that teaching students with limited or interrupted education should in no way be considered remedial, which in our experience is a common tendency among both educators and administrators. It is not the case that these students have "missed" learning something the first, second, or third time it was taught to them, but rather that they have never had the opportunity to learn the content or skills in the first place nor had the opportunity to develop the necessary and expected literacy and academic language. Therefore, while we strongly advocate adapting material and content, this does not mean it should be watered or dumbed down. When teachers have high expectations of their students and make these expectations clear to them, students benefit (Cavazos, 2009; Lukas, Henze, & Donato, 1990). An essential part of our approach is realizing that low or no literacy, limited English proficiency, and a lack of content knowledge should not be equated with limited cognitive development. SLIFE have the potential to develop these areas given the opportunity and can benefit substantially from instruction that meets their needs while helping them transition to the exigencies of schooling in the United States.

In addition to providing a general framework for pedagogical practices, *Breaking New Ground* centers on the intersection of culture, language, and pedagogy. An understanding of culture (e.g., DeCapua & Wintergerst, 2004; Wurzel, 2005) and how it impacts on an array of values, beliefs, behaviors, norms, and attitudes is essential for educators working with SLIFE. It is this cultural dimension that we believe has been neglected in most treatments of pedagogy for this population. Culturally responsive teaching and culturally relevant materials and curriculum can contribute to the lessening of disaffection and alienation that students may experience. However, without attention to deeper levels of culture that drive views of learning and knowing, we cannot ultimately decrease their cultural dissonance sufficiently for SLIFE to reach their academic potential.

The book as a whole provides a complete presentation of our instructional model from theory to practice and guides readers throughout to reflect on each element of the model, why and how it is essential and effective, and how they can use it in their own teaching of SLIFE. The book is divided into the following sections: Chapters 1 through 3 lay the theoretical foundation and present the instructional model. Chapter 4 describes the implementation of the model in actual classroom settings. Chapter 5 introduces project-based learning and examines how such an approach best lends itself to the full realization of our instructional model. Chapters 6 and 7 discuss project-based learning, the execution of projects in the instructional model, and comprehensive examples of projects. The text concludes with Chapter 8, a reflective chapter. Each chapter concludes with a section titled *For Further Exploration,* which describes a variety of activities designed to help readers reflect on and apply concepts and themes introduced in that chapter. In most chapters readers will also find short activities placed throughout that are relevant to a particular theme introduced in a given section.

Chapter 1 explores what culture is; how it affects the way people understand, interpret, and interact with the world around them; and how this in turn influences the learning environment and pedagogical practices. We frame the discussion by examining key cultural dimensions that impact education, such as individualism and collectivism. Understanding these dimensions of culture prepares teachers to facilitate the transition of these students to learning within a very different educational setting with its own culturally based values, assumptions, and behaviors.

Chapter 2 clarifies some of the fundamental assumptions about learning in U.S. schools and contrasts them with those of other types of learners, such as SLIFE. We conceptualize and describe the conflicting culturally based learning paradigms of SLIFE and those of U.S. mainstream education. Educators, as products of the dominant U.S. educational system, are seldom aware of what their educational values and assumptions are because they take them for granted. We make these explicit in the text so that readers achieve a better appreciation of who they themselves are as educators and who their learners are, and where they are coming from intellectually and culturally.

After the exploration of the contrasting learning paradigms of SLIFE and mainstream U.S. education, in Chapter 3 we introduce our instructional model, the **M**utually **A**daptive **L**earning **P**aradigm (MALP). This instructional model aids the shift for this population from the preferred learning paradigm to that of U.S schooling. The chapter outlines how, in order to accomplish this shift, both teachers and students must make adaptations and develop new perspectives and behaviors with regard to their respective roles. MALP explicitly incorporates cultural factors in learning and teaching, thereby reducing the cultural dissonance this population experiences in mainstream U.S. schooling.

The discussion then moves to explore a hands-on approach to implementing MALP in the classroom. Chapter 4 examines how MALP can be infused into lessons, using two teachers, Christina and Rick, to illustrate. In this chapter, readers see how MALP is implemented by these teachers of SLIFE in two different subject areas, social studies and math.

Taking the model from the lesson level to the project level, Chapter 5 explores project-based learning, and how and why it is essential to the implementation of the MALP instructional model. Building on this chapter, Chapter 6 explores four projects that specifically target academic learning activities, a key component of MALP. Chapter 7 continues with project-based learning by taking one project, *Class Surveys*, and offering a step-by-step discussion of how the project is implemented in the classroom, following the guidelines of MALP.

The text concludes with Chapter 8, a reflective chapter in which we revisit and reexamine the cultural assumptions underlying teaching and learning. This last chapter also includes sample lessons from a teacher both before and after she received training in MALP. Finally, readers will find observations from a former SLIFE who was successful in making the transition to formal education.

In sum, *Breaking New Ground* provides readers with a new understanding of the SLIFE population, introduces them to a new instructional model, and teaches them how to address the needs of their students using project-based learning infused with MALP.

1

Culture, Literacy, and Learning

THIS CHAPTER EXPLORES THE IMPLICATIONS for educating SLIFE in U.S. high schools. The perspective taken here is a cultural one. We firmly believe that the cultural dimension has all too often been neglected in addressing the educational issues. Yet, it is understanding the cultural dimension that we find to be key to promoting the academic success of SLIFE in U.S. school systems. We begin by examining what culture is and considering how culture influences learning. Next, we examine the role of literacy as part of the acculturation process and what literacy means for students who bring an oral orientation to communication and learning. Finally, we look at an underlying cultural dynamic common to SLIFE that impacts their ability to benefit from formal education and literacy in the context of the U.S. educational system.

What Is Culture?

Successful teachers understand the interplay of language and culture and how culture influences learning and teaching (Chavajay & Rogoff, 2002). Culture matters. Participation in one's culture influences patterns of human development. How and what one learns, and what one does with that knowledge, is the result of the cultural practices and traditions of one's community, or subculture (Spring, 2008).

Most people have a general sense of what culture is; yet, when asked to define *culture,* they often have difficulty defining it precisely because a large part of what comprises culture is below the level of conscious awareness. Culture is frequently perceived as referring to modes of dress, types of food, ways of greeting, and so on. These elements are, however, only the readily visible elements of culture. Culture also encompasses subconscious elements, such as values, beliefs, norms, and ways of both interpreting and understanding the world around us (Triandis 1995; Samovar & Porter, 2008).

Culture itself is not something innate, but rather something that is molded through collective and individual experiences (Triandis, 2000). DeCapua & Wintergerst (2004) define culture as

> the set of fundamental ideas, practices, and experiences shared by a group of people [and a] set of shared beliefs, norms, and attitudes that are used to guide the behaviors of a group of people, [and] to explain the world around them. (p. 11)

These cultural fundamentals are less immediately evident than the visible ele- ments of culture and can be termed *the invisible culture*. Taken together, the two parts of culture—visible culture and invisible culture—are often referred to as the **iceberg model of culture** (see Figure 1.1).

Those aspects of culture that are readily apparent and obvious, such as cuisine, architecture, music, clothing, and artifacts, form the part of the iceberg visible above water. Those that are below the level of conscious awareness, such as beliefs, values, norms, and assumptions, are underwater and less easily seen. Only a small percentage of what is culture is "above water" or visible. The larger part of culture is that which is not easily visible. It is these aspects of culture that affect how members of a culture interpret the world and the behaviors of others around them, as well as influencing priorities, the nature of relationships, social interactions, and pedagogical practices, both with respect to teaching and to learning (DeCapua & McDonell, 2008). Cultural values, norms, and beliefs lead members of a given cultural group to have worldviews and behaviors distinct from members of other groups.

In the following vignette, *The Chopsticks,* notice how the father teaches his chil- dren about a significant value in their culture.

The Chopsticks

After you read this story, write your thoughts about it.

My brother and I were arguing over a trivial issue. We both stormed off, convinced we would never get along, never be friends; we wished the other was never born, or, better yet, adopted, for we wanted no relation to the other. My father, angry, dragged us down to the kitchen table and placed two chopsticks in front of us. He asked us each to choose one and see if we could break it, to which we complied. It was an easy task, breaking a simple stick of wood. Then, though, he bound together four chopsticks with a rubber band, each chopstick representing a member of our immediate family. He handed the chopstick bundle to my brother and dared him to break it. Angered and hot headed, my brother grabbed the chopsticks and, in a fury, pushed and pulled and wiggled and smashed those chopsticks, but to no avail. One chopstick, my father explained, is very weak, but together, as a family, we could withstand everything. My brother and I nodded in agreement as our anger, for the most part, had passed. At that moment, I believed my father was simply teaching me that I needed to try harder to get along with my brother. Years later, though, this memory has endured, and I realize that this was not simply a lesson for the moment, but a larger cultural value my father was trying to instill in his children. The family unit is more important than our individual selves; it is only through the strength of family that we can achieve and persevere.

—Nicole

FIGURE 1.1   The Iceberg Model of Culture

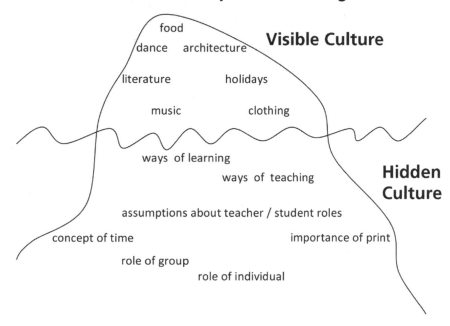

Culture Model: Tip of the Iceberg

food
dance   architecture   **Visible Culture**
literature   holidays
music   clothing

ways of learning
ways of teaching   **Hidden Culture**

assumptions about teacher / student roles
concept of time   importance of print
role of group
role of individual

Adapted from Ting-Toomey & Chung (2005).

Individualism versus Collectivism

Culture is the active participation of individuals in the practices, traditions, values, and behaviors of a culture (Spring, 2008). People generally consider themselves to be members of a cultural group that can be referred to as their majority culture. At the same time, people are members of myriad subcultures, which can be based on any variety of factors, such as ethnicity, region, community of practices, or societal roles. Despite these subcultural and certainly individual differences, there are salient cultural aspects that can and have been identified for different cultures. There are fewer within-cultural differences and variations than there are cross-cultural ones (Cuellar, Arnold, & Gonzalez, 1995; Lustig & Koester, 2009).

The major cultural dimension relevant to our examination of SLIFE is collectivism versus individualism. Cultures can be classified as primarily closer to one or the other category along a continuum that is based on the role and priorities of the individual in a given culture. In a collectivistic culture, people view themselves as integral parts of networks, or extended groups. These networks are generally based on kinship but may also be based on clan, religious, or other ties viewed as essential to identifying who belongs to a particular group (Hofstede, 2001). In individualistic cultures, in contrast, people view themselves as independent actors focused on their identity as separate individuals (Kim, 1994; Triandis, 1995).

Collectivistic Cultures

In collectivistic cultures, people's sense of who they are, their obligations and responsibilities, the demands placed on them, and their sense of well-being are influenced
by their place and role within their network. Who one is as an individual is not as
important as who one is in relationship to everyone else, and commitments to one's
network take precedence over individual needs and desires. The focus is on the group
rather than on the individual, meaning that self-actualization, personal attributes, and
the accomplishments of an individual for his or her own sake are not central (Gardner,
Gabriel, & Lee, 1999).

Instead, the actions of an individual are viewed in terms of how they reflect,
benefit, or contribute to one's group (Oyserman & Lee, 2008; Triandis, 2000). Asian
and Latin American immigrant adolescents, for instance, are more concerned with
their obligations to their families than are mainstream adolescents of European backgrounds (Fuligini, Tseng, & Lam, 1999). Mexican parents in the U.S. are often shocked
by strict school attendance policies, believing that extended absences to the family's
home country are both justified and necessary for such family matters as death, illness,
celebrating holidays, or other matters and that they should take priority over school
attendance (Olmedo, 2003).

Individualistic Cultures

Members of individualistic cultures give priority to personal goals, efforts, achievements,
and independence. A person's identity depends primarily on individual attributes,
traits, and accomplishments, and one's sense of well-being centers on self-actualization
and one's own performance. Personal judgments and decisions rather than group decisions are the norm. Children, for example, are encouraged to pursue personal interests.
College students generally choose their majors based on what they want to do rather
than what is the best choice for their family. Personal responsibility and accountability
are paramount, and less emphasis is placed on one's identity as part of a network with
mutually reciprocal obligations and responsibilities (Hofstede, 2001; Toth & Xu, 1999).

The following vignette, *Praise*, illustrates a difference in perspective on appropriate teacher behavior between collectivistic and individualistic cultures.

Praise

The teacher, seeing how much progress Lea has made on her part of an autobiography project, points it out to the other students in the class and tells them that this is
really good work, indicating different parts as she praises Lea's efforts. She then suggests that if they have any concerns about doing their parts, they should ask Lea for
help. Meanwhile, Lea, embarrassed, keeps her eyes down and, as soon as the bell rings,
hurriedly leaves the classroom. The other students leave more slowly, chatting, and
laughing with each other.

1. **Were the teacher's actions appropriate?**

2. **Why or why not? Explain, and share your comments.**

A Continuum—Not a Dichotomy

In any discussion of individualism and collectivism, it is important to remember that these two complex constructs are not mutually exclusive and do not represent a strict dichotomy of cultural differences. Rather, the individualism-collectivism dimension, as previously stated, should be regarded as a continuum of cultural differences with subcultural differences and variations (Green, Deschamps, & Páez, 2005; Kagitçibasi, 1994).

Even within any given majority culture, we can observe elements of both collectivism and individualism (Oyserman, Coon, & Kemmelmeier, 2002; Tyler et al., 2008). No culture is completely homogeneous. Some members of an individualistic culture will more strongly embrace characteristics of individualism than will others. Nevertheless, in an individualistic culture, the majority of persons will have individualistic attributes and in a collectivistic culture, the majority will have collectivistic attributes (see Figure 1.2).

The two overlapping bell-type curves in Figure 1.3 (on page 16) illustrate the nature of the continuum from collectivistic to individualistic. Cultures generally exist within a range on this continuum, and individuals within a culture find themselves anywhere along that range. The peaks of the two curves represent the largest concentration of individuals in each of the two intersecting cultural categories. For example, members of Mexican culture, who are typically within the collectivistic range, may be toward the collectivistic end of the continuum, but they may also fall so far toward the individualistic end that they overlap with members of individualistic cultures. The reverse is true for members of the U.S. culture, who may be at either end of the individualistic range on the continuum.

Care must be taken when applying labels to humans and cultures to avoid overgeneralizations and stereotyping. Despite general salient cultural aspects for the larger notion of culture, it is very important that teachers of SLIFE not lose sight of the fact that their students are also members of specific communities and subcultures. Nevertheless, we cannot discount the importance of understanding the cultural divide

---

FIGURE 1.2   Bell Curves of Culture

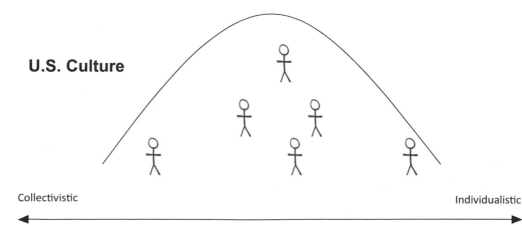

Collectivistic   Individualistic

FIGURE 1.3   The Intersection of Collectivistic and Individualistic Attributes

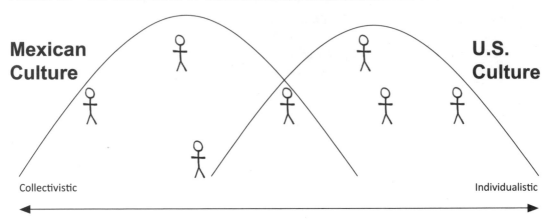

Mexican Culture   **U.S. Culture**

Collectivistic   Individualistic

between individualism and collectivism, and the attendant cultural values influencing the attitudes and assumptions as manifested in accepted classroom practices and behaviors (Rothstein-Fisch et al., 2003). It has been estimated that more than 70 percent of the world's cultures are collectivistic (Triandis, 1995). Given that the majority of immigrants to the U.S. come from collectivistic cultures in Asia, Latin America, and Africa, it is likely that most SLIFE whom teachers will encounter are from collectivistic cultures. Because there are salient cultural values that distinguish collectivistic and individualistic cultures, U.S. teachers may find SLIFE engaging in unexpected behaviors.

As an example, consider the concept of *cooperative learning*. In the U.S., cooperative learning is hailed as an effective "best practice" in promoting student engagement and learning for all populations (see, e.g., Echevarria, Vogt, & Short, 2008; McMaster & Fuchs, 2002). Cooperative learning, extensively researched and discussed in the educational field, is structured around basic tenets teachers are to follow to ensure that group work is carefully structured. As DeCapua & Marshall (2011) point out, this could be considered a collectivistic practice. However, teachers' perceptions and understanding of how students are to perform in group settings are what make it a reflection of the individualism of mainstream U.S. culture. In classrooms when learning is conducted cooperatively, it is viewed as a team effort. Each person is assigned a specific role or task that, when fulfilled by all the members of the group, completes the group assignment. Each member acts as an individual member of the team and is individually accountable for his or her own learning (Morrison, 2009). From a collectivistic viewpoint, in contrast, when a group operates cooperatively, members reach consensus and share both the responsibility and the accountability for the group's tasks, not needing to specify individual contributions (Ibarra, 2001).

An example of a country whose culture in general is far more collectivistic than U.S. mainstream culture is Mexico, accounting for about 30 percent of all immigrants to the United States (Passel & Cohn, 2009). Mexican culture has a strong emphasis on the extended familial network. Cultural values include prioritizing reciprocal obligations and support and the needs of the family when making individual decisions (Cauce & Domenech-Rodríguez, 2002). The term *familismo* is often used to refer to how strongly the family is revered in Mexican culture (Rodriguez, Mira, Paez, & Myers, 2007). In families with limited economic resources, children dropping out of school to help the family, whether by working and providing additional income or by caring for younger family members, is not uncommon, reflecting the priority of one's group needs over individual wants or desires.

Review The Chopsticks

1. Review the notes you made on *The Chopsticks* (page 12).

2. Share these thoughts with others.

3. After your discussion and after having read more of this chapter, how have your thoughts changed?

4. How might you use *The Chopsticks* and what you learned in this section to explain examples of collectivistic behavior to other teachers, administrators, and/or support personnel?

In sum, many SLIFE come from collectivistic cultures with very different beliefs, assumptions, and expectations from those in an individualistic culture such as the U.S. We now turn to an examination of an equally important common characteristic—pragmatic ways of thinking about the world and about learning.

How Does Culture Influence Learning?

Formal Education

In considering the challenge that SLIFE face in encountering formal education, often for the first time, we need to define what is understood by the term *formal education.* Formal education occurs within a specific structure—that is, a regulated and predetermined school system. *Informal education,* in contrast, is seen as incidental learning— that is, learning that takes place in response to needs as they come up. SLIFE often come to U.S. schools with rich experiences and other types of informal learning experiences. None of these, however, prepare them for the formal education that they will encounter in the United States. Therefore, in order to assist them, the first step is to understand the particular model of formal education prevalent in the schools where SLIFE will find themselves: Western-style education. The so-called Western-style model rests on certain principles that drive instruction and that influence educators, often without their explicitly realizing that they are so influenced. These principles derive from ways of thinking that, in turn, result in specific cultural perspectives on learning.

Pragmatic and Academic Ways of Thinking

Culture influences the learning process with respect to both how people learn and what they value as part of learning (August, Goldenberg, & Rueda, 2006; Needham, 2003). As Hall (1976) explains:

> Education and educational systems are about as laden with emotion and as characteristic of a given culture as its language . . . It seems inconceivable to the average person brought up in one culture that something as basic as [education] could be done any differently from the way they themselves were taught . . . This is because, in the process of learning they have acquired a long set of tacit conditions and assumptions in which learning is embedded. (p. 47)

The Western-style model of education is predicated on formal problem solving and scientific reasoning, drawing on print and using formally trained teachers (Gutiérrez & Rogoff, 2003). Flynn (2007) cogently discusses the differences between those who have extensively participated in such a model of education and those who have not. The Western-style model is built on scientific conventions and is characterized by problem solving on a formal level and by abstract reasoning separated from the concrete world and real-life experiences. It is referred to in this text as **academic ways of thinking**, demonstrated in the following activity.

TEST YOUR KNOWLEDGE

Answer these questions.

1. What do dogs and rabbits have in common?
2. What is a tree?
3. a. Washington, DC, is the capital of the U.S.   True   False
    b. New York City is the capital of New York State.   True   False

---

Those readers who answered "mammals," "fur," "ears," "paws," "They're animals," or anything similar to Question 1 used abstract, scientific categories of classification. For Question 2, readers who answered "something with a trunk and limbs" or "something that has branches and leaves" or anything along these lines were again defining based on abstract scientific ways of looking at the world. Teachers across disciplines and in all grade levels spend a great deal of time asking students for formal definitions (Schleppegrell, 2004; Snow, Cancini, González, & Shriberg, 1989), as in Questions 1 and 2. This is a teaching technique common in U.S. classrooms but unfamiliar to SLIFE and one that is revisited in later chapters. For Question 3, readers most likely had no difficulty recognizing how to answer a true/false question, even if they were not necessarily certain of the answer to Question 3b (which is false).

What the responses to the questions in this activity demonstrate is a familiarity with abstract, scientific, or academic reasoning, derived from the fact that readers of this text have spent many years participating successfully in Western-style schooling. SLIFE, however, have different ways of looking at and understanding the world. For Question 1, for instance, they are likely to respond with something like, "You use a dog to hunt a rabbit" or "People eat dogs and rabbits," or even "They don't have anything in common" because they are focused on the concrete and on functional relationships (Flynn, 2007). With respect to Question 2, SLIFE often wonder why they are being asked to define something that is obvious. From their pragmatic perspective, trees are everywhere, so what is the point of asking what a tree is. Finally, for Question 3, the entire notion of true/false is perplexing. If something is false, why mention it? A false statement is pointless (Lujan, 2008). As products of 16-plus years of an educational model that poses such questions routinely, teachers are rarely aware of the cultural assumptions underlying them. From the point of Western-style education, there is an academic way of interpreting the world, which is assumed to be the correct and the "right way." Yet, this type of thinking is very different from the pragmatic way of those who have not engaged in such formal learning.

As Flynn (2007) observes, at a concrete level, knowing that all toadstools are poisonous, a person finding a toadstool will associate poison with toadstool and therefore avoid it. In addition to being concrete knowledge, it is knowledge that has immediate and immutable practical real-world relevance: Eat the wrong type of mushroom and it will kill you. Knowing how to classify dogs and rabbits together, on the other hand, is based on an abstract level of thinking derived from scientific classification, in this case having learned that the class *mammal* is one characterized by live births, milk-producing mammary glands in females for nourishing the young, and hair. There is no immediate relevance for this knowledge, but part of the Western-style education process is learning abstractions, logic, and the hypothetical, all of which are detached from real-world applications.

Beginning no later than kindergarten, U.S. school instruction revolves around categorization, classification, and other abstract thinking far removed from concrete and functional referents. At even earlier ages, children in the U.S. begin learning with songs such as Sesame Street's "One of These Things Is Not Like the Others." The objective of such activities is to group like items into a category and to name that category, without regard to any type of contextualization (DeCapua & Marshall, 2010a). Table 1.1 illustrates some of the principal differences between pragmatic knowledge and academic knowledge.

For students accustomed to pragmatic ways of thinking and learning, the notion of "knowledge for knowledge's sake" is often peculiar because for them, learning has immediate, practical, concrete relevance (DeCapua & Marshall, 2010a). Children

TABLE 1.1
Pragmatic Knowledge versus Academic Knowledge

Pragmatic Knowledge	Academic Knowledge
Based on experience, often accumulated over generations and passed down orally	Based on logic and the hypothetical
Focused on the concrete, functional	Focused on abstractions—e.g,. taxonomies, comparison/contrast
Concerned with immediate relevance, benefit	Immediate relevance and benefit not necessarily important
Frequently culture/environment specific	Not tied to specific culture or environment—e.g., algebraic equations, definition of a mammal
Changeable	Relatively static

learn by observation and participating in ongoing tasks, thus providing immediate relevance to their learning. They attend to and practice tasks of direct relevance and receive immediate feedback, whether explicit or implicit, from adults or more adept older children (González, et al., 1995; Rogoff, 2003). These tasks include childcare, agricultural practices, pottery making, weaving, automobile repair, masonry, and more.

Pragmatic ways of thinking and learning contrast with much of Western-style education where an assumed goal of K–12 instruction is to prepare students for successful future participation in the adult world of work and life (Morrison, 2009). Learning is separated from life and delegated to a specific institution, the school. For SLIFE, on the other hand, learning comes through participation in the daily activities of life, and from an early age they observe and join in family and community labors and endeavors. Thus, while high school SLIFE may have much real-world knowledge based on their life experiences and are well able to interpret and organize new knowledge from a pragmatic perspective, unfamiliarity with academic ways of learning and understanding the world disadvantages them in U.S. mainstream classrooms (DeCapua & Marshall, 2010a, 2010b; Marshall & DeCapua, 2011).

Assumptions and Culturally Based Pedagogy

The cultural dimensions of individualism and academic ways of thinking are reflected in expectations and assumptions about teaching and learning. Most teachers in U.S. schools, given the nature of their professional training and their own schooling experiences, hold specific subconscious assumptions about pedagogy, learning, and student and teacher behaviors. Mainstream students, especially by the time they are in high school, share similar assumptions.

The following activity provides an opportunity to explore such assumptions.

AGREE OR DISAGREE

Consider these statements and decide whether or not you agree with them. Circle A if you agree. Circle D if you disagree.

1. Students come to school wanting to excel and distinguish themselves.   A   D

2. Students want to be independent as learners.   A   D

3. The school experience should prepare students for their future.   A   D

4. Teachers should help students become independent.   A   D

5. Students expect to be individually accountable for their work.   A   D

6. Students expect to perform learning tasks for the teacher to evaluate.   A   D

7. Students should be singled out and praised for good work.   A   D

Readers who agreed with some or all of these statements are reflecting the cultural assumptions underlying the Western-style educational model of which they most likely are a product and in which they are, or will be, participating as an educator. In fact, these assumptions are not universally held and are not the same assumptions as most SLIFE bring with them to U.S. schools. These cultural assumptions of education will be discussed in greater detail in Chapter 2.

Pedagogical theories and practices are rooted in cultural beliefs, norms, values, and assumptions (Spring, 2008). The teacher as an authority figure and arbiter of knowledge is more common in a culture in which hierarchical roles and respect for authority dominate (Triandis, 1994; 1995). Returning to the iceberg theory of culture, we can see that most of the beliefs, norms, values, and assumptions underlying culture are below the level of conscious awareness. Educators are frequently unaware of how much of pedagogical theories and practices are based in fundamental beliefs and to what extent these pervade education (Cole, 1998; Spring, 2008). Indeed, the most difficult cultural assumptions and beliefs to examine are those that are central to one's culture. For example, the popular North American pedagogical belief that students should be active participants in their learning derives from American cultural preferences for action and doing (Needham, 2003). This belief in students as active learners differs from the predominant pedagogical beliefs usually found in traditional collectivistic and hierarchical cultures, such as Cambodian or Chinese culture (K.H. Kim, 2005). In such cultures, pedagogical practices emphasize respect for the authority and wisdom of the teacher. Teachers are repositories of knowledge, and it is their duty to impart this knowledge to their students, whose duty, in turn, is to receive and absorb this knowledge.

To take another example, many Latino immigrants come from collectivistic cultures. For them, it is more important to work together to help others accomplish classroom tasks first and then turn their attention to their own tasks. Such behavior often conflicts with the U.S. focus on individual accountability and achievement (Rothstein-Fisch et al., 2003). As shown in the earlier discussion of cooperative learning, teachers expect individual contributions, even in group work where collaboration is fostered. In the United States, a central assumption of teachers is that K–12 instruction should produce independent learners—that is, students who know how to learn or gain information on their own, use what they have learned, and be able to apply their knowledge and skills to new learning situations (Joyce, Weil, & Calhoun, 2009). Scaffolding, for example, is considered an essential component of effective instruction for all learners. This is the notion that teachers promote learning by providing students with needed support for learning. As students become more knowledgeable and confident and develop their ability to learn independently, the teacher removes this support little by little (Cazden, 1988; Gibbons, 2002). The concept of the independent learner is closely tied to an individualistic society with an educational system that values learning on one's own.

This chart highlights some of the core values of U.S. mainstream education and representative pedagogical practices.

CORE VALUES AND PRACTICES

Core Value	Representative Pedagogical Practices
K–12 instruction should produce independent learners.	• Scaffolding: provide support for learning as needed, gradually removing the support as students learn to depend on themselves • Asking for assistance or giving assistance only when necessary
Students are individually responsible and accountable for their learning.	• Cooperative work means working together but with each person individually accountable for a specific task and/or product • Individual assessment of material learned, often through standardized tests
School prepares learner for life after school.	• Designing curriculum without immediate real-world relevance

Literacy

In combination with collectivism and pragmatic ways of thinking, SLIFE commonly bring with them an oral culture, rooted not in literacy practices but in the oral transmission of knowledge. Not only do SLIFE face new ways of thinking about learning, they must master a tool considered essential to Western-style formal education: the printed word. Literacy skills have embedded themselves so deeply in our educational system that it is difficult to conceive of a successful school experience devoid of these skills. However, SLIFE may have learned a great deal in their lives without this tool. In their world, they have succeeded in becoming learned and competent in many areas. Such knowledge, referred to by Moll and Greenberg (1990) as "funds of knowledge," exists in their memories and in those of others they rely on for their expertise. SLIFE think of other people as their primary resources for knowledge rather than the printed word—people supply knowledge directly through oral interaction.

Once in our schools, however, learning without this tool—literacy—is not a viable option. In order to understand the challenge and to appreciate people's views of learning through literacy, the notion of literacy is examined more closely.

As teachers, literacy is deeply embedded in our processes for interacting with information; therefore, you very likely had negative feelings, including frustration, disorientation, anger, helplessness, and anxiety, in response to the situation. Even those teachers who rely heavily on auditory channels still expect visual cues, specifically print, as a support.

No Pencils, No Books shows how literacy is more than a skill or a process; it is an integral part of our culture, and embracing literacy is part of the acculturation process of SLIFE to U.S. schooling.

No Pencils, No Books

Imagine yourself at a professional development event with your colleagues. The speaker has just announced that there will be no printed words either on slides or handouts. Moreover, there will be no note taking. In fact, you have been instructed to put down all writing implements for the duration of the presentation. Finally, no tape recording is permitted.

1. **How would you feel?**
2. **Take a moment to write some words to describe your emotional reaction to such a situation.**

What Is Literacy?

Literacy is a social practice that is critically connected to people's social identities; thus, when they develop literacy, they also learn new values, norms, and different ways of thinking (Gee, 1996). Over the years, there has been a major shift in the understanding of literacy: Although it was previously identified as the ability to encode and decode print, it is now viewed as the appropriate knowledge and skills to communicate and extract meaning through a variety of socially situated and rapidly changing media (Hawkins, 2004; Kress, 2003).

Good teaching does not automatically result in academic success. Teachers must make direct connections to the realities of students' lives and their need for immediate benefit in order for them to see value in literacy (Hawkins, 2004; Sarroub, Pernicek, & Sweeney, 2007). As work by Luis González and associates has shown (1995; 2005), conventional literacy activities often fail to motivate and engage students, while activities that teachers base on students' language, culture, and communities are more successful. These findings support the notion of the underlying social nature of literacy (Street, 2007).

Often there is a lack of textbooks and other print resources in the home countries of SLIFE, with a concomitant emphasis on rote learning (Harger, 2008). Generally speaking, teachers write information on a chalkboard that students then copy into their notebooks or onto slate or whiteboards (DeCapua, Smathers, & Tang, 2009). SLIFE are not accustomed to turning to print as a resource for learning, and it takes time and effort to orient SLIFE toward books and other printed materials. Moreover, the ubiquity of printed materials in the general environment and literacy resources typically found in most U.S. middle class homes is not part of the world of SLIFE—there are few or no traditional print materials such as magazines, newspapers, books, flyers, or newsletters, and rarely a computer (Richardson et al., 2007).

A SLIFE once commented to one of us that before coming to the United States, there had never been any need for him to read:

> I live village, nothing for read, no sign, no book. I go school, we read what teacher write but I ask why learn read if no something to read. Here I walk street, everywhere read. Before I no need reading but here everything is read.
>
> —Sergio, El Salvador

This student experiences a common reaction SLIFE have when coming to the U.S. While print previously played little or no role in their lives in school, they now must read and read to extract meaning. Thus, SLIFE need help transitioning from a world based on oral transmission to one based on print.

Another student said:

> The most importants I have learned about the United States that is a book, newspapers, or notebook and pens. These things are always let me know how to live here. . . . I always remember the books are the most important things for me to learn when I live in the United States. (originally cited in DeCapua & Marshall, 2011, p. 35)
>
> —Vuong, Vietnam

SLIFE range from having had no exposure to the printed word to having had many years of exposure. What all SLIFE share, however, is that they arrive in U.S. schools thinking of printed material as distant from their own immediate concerns and not thinking of it as a tool for learning and for expressing one's thoughts. For many of them, learning to use print can be frustrating:

> I lived in a small village and didn't attend school. When I arrived at this high school in America I began attending school for the first time in my life. I feel very frustrated. I don't understand any of my teachers, I don't know how to read or write, I don't know the alphabet.
>
> —Yei (Minnesota Department of Children, Families & Learning, 2002, no page)

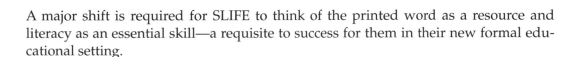

Review No Pencils, No Books

1. Take a moment to compare these quotes from SLIFE to your response to our earlier scenario on page 23.

2. What reactions did you experience to the student quotes?

3. Discuss how your perspective of literacy and the notion of print as an essential resource contrasts with the students' perspectives.

A major shift is required for SLIFE to think of the printed word as a resource and literacy as an essential skill—a requisite to success for them in their new formal educational setting.

SLIFE Achievement Gap or Cultural Dissonance?

So far, we have explored the three major cultural characteristics shared by most SLIFE. They are collectivistic, pragmatic, and oral in their orientation to the world around them and are likely to bring these cultural orientations with them to the United States and, subsequently, into their new educational setting. Considering the intersection of the cultural orientations of SLIFE with the expectations and assumptions of U.S. educators, we can predict that school will be difficult for them, as it is different or even new. Second, we can predict that learning to read and write will be challenging for SLIFE as these are new processes for them. Given the literacy demands of U.S. high school classrooms, SLIFE will experience an overwhelming sense of frustration in a formal educational setting. Third, we can predict that SLIFE will find the individualistic orientation and academic ways of thinking of U.S. schools to be difficult and to be what creates the most profound cultural clash.

In the interest of giving this feeling of intense frustration a name, researchers have defined cultural concepts that attempt to encapsulate the difficulties faced by these students or other groups of students whose experiences and backgrounds differ substantially from what is expected and required in their new school setting. In the literature these differences between home experiences and school experiences have been identified as *cultural discontinuity* (e.g., Gay, 2000; Nieto, 1994; Tyler et al., 2008) and as *cultural dissonance* (e.g., Gordon & Yowell,1999; Ladson-Billings, 1995; Ibarra, 2001). Here we use the term **cultural dissonance** to describe the mismatch between home and school when SLIFE, who come from different cultural values and different learning paradigms, encounter the mainstream cultural values and learning paradigm of U.S. schools. This mismatch frequently causes feelings of isolation, confusion, disengagement, and inadequacy (Sarroub, Pernicek, & Sweeney, 2007; Schlosser, 1992). The experience of cultural dissonance can have a negative effect on student performance, leading to poor academic achievement and high dropout rates (Gordon & Yowell, 1999; Tyler et al., 2008).

It has been argued that the academic failure of ELLs is due to the cultural dissonance they encounter when entering U.S. schools (see, e.g., Gay, 2000; Nieto, 2004). SLIFE, by virtue of having limited or interrupted formal education, face even greater cultural dissonance. The position taken in this text is that it is this dissonance that is responsible for the lack of school success and concomitant high dropout rates we see among SLIFE. Therefore, rather than label their failure as a gap in **achievement**, focusing on performance and ability, we view it as a **cultural** gap, resulting from acute cultural dissonance. Viewed thus, SLIFE no longer appear as failing students when judged against a standard of an unfamiliar set of principles, practices, and perspectives, but rather as emerging intercultural agents who are embarking on a new venture and who can be guided along the way by knowledgeable, culturally aware educators. One of the goals of this book is to introduce a new instructional model, one that teachers can use to build bridges between pragmatic ways of thinking and academic ways of thinking to respond to the cultural gap and decrease the cultural dissonance experienced by SLIFE.

For Further Exploration

1. Write five to ten sentences briefly describing what you believe makes a good student and how you think students learn best. After you have finished, share your thoughts with a partner or in small groups. What were the similarities and what were the differences in all the philosophies? To what might you attribute these similarities and differences?

2. Go back to the questions on page 18. Try to ask at least five different people two of these questions: "What do dogs and rabbits have in common?" and "What is a tree?" How do your results compare to the discussion after the questions on page 18.

3. Thinking about your own background and cultural orientation through the lens presented here, try to place yourself on the continuum from collectivistic to individualistic. Explain why you placed yourself where you did on the continuum. Compare your results with a partner. What trends do you see? Explain.

4. If you are a practicing teacher, think about your students. How would you place them along this collectivistic/individualistic continuum based on the examples and information provided throughout the chapter? Compare the results. What trends do you see?

5. Observe a classroom with SLIFE, and take notes on the behaviors and interactions of these students. In particular, look for those that illustrate the points made in this chapter about literacy, culture, and formal education. Share your impressions with a partner or in small groups.

2

Two Different Learning Paradigms

Activity A: Familiar Ways of Thinking
Recite the months of the year to yourself.

Activity B: Unfamiliar Ways of Thinking
Now recite the months of the year to yourself in alphabetical order.

FOR ACTIVITY A, YOU PROBABLY RATTLED OFF *January, February, March, April,* and so on until you reached *December*. For Activity B, you probably were able to recite the months in alphabetical order, but not without thinking about it for a while or even resorting to listing the months and then placing them in alphabetical order. This is an illustration of a *formal schema*. We have learned to store the months of the year in our brain in chronological order beginning with the first month of the calendar year and ending with the last one. When we are asked to retrieve them alphabetically, it is difficult to do so, because the request does not match our formal schema (James, 1987).

Formal schema in reading and writing normally refers to the rhetorical organization of text. Research in this area by Carrell and others (see, e.g., Carrell, 1998; Grabe & Stoller, 2002) has focused on the importance of this type of schema in addition to the content schema about the topic of the text. In our work, we return to the definition of schema from Alderson (2000) and Anderson (1999) in which a schema theory of learning can refer more broadly to how one stores concepts regarding how we experience and interact with the world in which we live. By extension, we see learning as it is exemplified in Western-style classroom settings as based on a set of concepts that can be described as a cluster of **formal schemata**. If one is unfamiliar with these schemata for how education takes place, one may not be able to access or take advantage of the educational opportunities provided. This is similar to what many SLIFE face when entering the U.S. educational system. They are entering the school system with very different schemata and do not organize and process information the same way that U.S. high school students do.

Returning to the iceberg metaphor from Chapter 1, we note that in our discussion of learning we are looking at cultural aspects that lie beneath the surface, rather than the cultural differences commonly considered when teachers seek to educate in a culturally sensitive manner. Just as SLIFE bring expectations for learning with them, the teachers they encounter also have their expectations about learning in a classroom setting. For the most part, these expectations reflect mainstream U.S. cultural values derived from the European worldviews of earlier immigrant groups (Gay, 2000; Nieto, 2010). Often these values are assumed and not articulated. In this chapter, we look at these expectations from a contrastive perspective, which allows us to observe how cultural dissonance occurs when SLIFE enter our schools and attempt to learn there.

Conceptualizing a Learning Paradigm

Based on our discussion of the SLIFE population in U.S. schools and our examination of the close relationship between culture and learning, we can clearly see how a framework for approaching learning would assist us in adequately serving the needs of this at-risk group of students. The conceptualization of learning used in this book is comprised of three components, each of which contributes to an overall learning paradigm, or way of organizing and thinking about learning in a given setting. These three components are: conditions for learning, processes for learning, and activities for learning. Taken together, these three components can describe the learning experience of SLIFE.

Components of a Learning Paradigm

A. Conditions for learning
B. Processes for learning
C. Activities for learning

Component A, **conditions for learning,** refers to differing underlying expectations about learning and teaching assumed by both students and their teachers in any given culture or subculture. Component B, **processes for learning,** refers to how students develop, retain, and display their learning. As we will explore in this chapter, these processes differ greatly for SLIFE and for U.S. classrooms. Component C, **activities for learning,** refers to how different cultures and subcultures conceive of and interpret the world. Chapter 1 examined how ways of thinking differ depending on whether people have a pragmatic worldview or an academic worldview, the latter a result of Western-style schooling.

The conditions, processes, and activities most closely associated with SLIFE will be examined and then compared and contrasted with those commonly present in U.S. schools today. In doing this, we will examine the mismatch between what most SLIFE need and expect in a setting designed for learning and the reality in terms of what they find in the majority of U.S. classrooms.

Component A: Conditions for Learning in the Two Settings

In discussing cultural differences in Chapter 1, we examined collectivistic cultures, from which the majority of SLIFE come. In such cultures, given the primacy of group relationships and obligations, a feeling of interconnectedness is primary. In addition, as students coming from pragmatic worlds where learning is concrete and tied to their everyday lives, SLIFE are accustomed to learning that is immediately relevant to the real world. These two conditions—interconnectedness and immediate relevance—form Component A. SLIFE have had real-world experiences that have prepared them for daily living but that have not prepared them for Western-style schooling. They generally also have extended family or group ties that expect and encourage strong social relationships and responsibilities. These contrast with the conditions they find when they enter a U.S. classroom where the focus is on preparation for the future and where it is expected that the students are moving toward independence. Table 2.1 illustrates the conditions of the two learning paradigms.

Immediate Relevance versus Future Relevance

The first condition contrasts the way the learning paradigms view the relevance of what is being learned. In this case, the contrast is direct, namely immediate relevance versus future relevance. The underlying cultural condition is whether one's thinking is grounded in the present or is oriented toward the future. The first condition SLIFE seek is **immediate relevance,** so that what they learn will be applicable to their lives in the short term. Unlike mainstream U.S. students, who have begun school at a young age and been taught for years that school comes first and that when they grow up they will be educated for the U.S. work world (Morrison, 2009), most SLIFE are used to learning what they need to know when they need to know it. When teachers select material and justify the importance of the curriculum, they unintentionally create cultural dissonance for SLIFE by not taking into account their need to see the relevance of this material and the curriculum to their lives.

Teaching is an act of cultural transmission (Alexander, 2000; Gay, 2000; Trumbull et al., 2001). For more than a century, U.S. society has viewed the education of its children as of central concern. Educational issues appear frequently in the news, whether local or national. While there is no consensus as to what should and should not be taught, or on exactly how the instruction should be delivered or even who should pay for it, education is in the forefront of many people's minds.

TABLE 2.1
Component A: Conditions for Learning

SLIFE	U.S. Schools
Immediate relevance	Future relevance
Interconnectedness	Independence

The goal setting and planning that currently seems to drive U.S. schools demonstrates how teachers and learners focus on the future. Much, if not most, of the content that students actually learn is not retained in later years, but serves to develop their intellectual tools and broaden their minds. When teachers explain to students that they will need to know something, it is often accompanied by reference to some other future event, such as, "This will help you on the test" or "You need to know this because you'll be learning about [some related topic] later." Course sequences are another example. Like links in a chain, one course prepares students for the next, so that they know they will need what they learn today for another class they will take later. The expectation is that students need to focus on the task at hand in order to attain this future benefit. Learning is seen as a foundation for future experience, preceding "real" life, rather than paralleling it (Althen, 2002). The "real life" for which the child is being prepared may come long after the learning takes place.

While many teachers strive to make learning relevant to their students, there is an underlying assumption that doing so is a matter of added interest and motivation. Students understand that ultimately it is not the current relevance that is the priority, but the curriculum itself that will be assessed and that the teacher will build on in all their assignments and schoolwork.

For SLIFE, before they entered U.S. schools, learning took place in an immediately relevant situation where they would use what they were learning in the real world for a real-world task. As learners, they had become competent in the skills they needed to master for specific purposes in their environment. SLIFE are accustomed to learning what they need to know at the time they incorporate it into their daily life. For example, care of farm animals, planting of crops, or traditional handicrafts are learned by example and by doing. When a person learns cooking, agriculture, or carpentry skills, the new knowledge is applied at the time of learning. The learner observes, practices, and gets immediate feedback; learning is pragmatic and parallels life (Lave, 1996; Mejía et al., 2007).

Current theory in psychology postulates that all learning builds on transfer—that is, students' ability to see similarities between prior learning and the current situation, as well as being able to use their prior knowledge in new situations (Mestre, 2002). When material is relevant to learners it is more likely that they will be receptive to it and that they will be able to engage in this transfer. When SLIFE enter U.S. classrooms, their prior knowledge in many cases does not allow for transfer, unless teachers make explicit connections between their pragmatic way of thinking and classroom academic ways of thinking. Teachers must consciously strive to incorporate the pragmatic knowledge of their students and their students' communities into their classroom and curriculum. Contributing to the sense of cultural dissonance that SLIFE experience in U.S. schools is the fact that much of secondary school curriculum is necessarily academic in nature, not relevant or related to the pragmatic worldviews of SLIFE, and has no context relative to their lives. Experiencing this cultural dissonance makes them vulnerable to "educational disadvantage" with consequent negative affects on academic achievement (Gordon & Yowell, 1999; Nieto, 1994).

When SLIFE do feel connected to the content being presented or the skills being taught, they are more likely to engage since it will parallel their prior learning experiences (DeCapua & Marshall, 2010b; Marshall & DeCapua, 2010; Marshall,

DeCapua, & Antolini, 2010). In addition to the importance of immediate relevance, SLIFE also seek a personal connection, a feeling of being interconnected to the other people with whom they are sharing the learning experiences.

Interconnectedness versus Independence

The second key element of Component A highlights the contrast in how individuals from different cultures view themselves in relation to others in the learning setting. Here again, the difference is a major one, as expressed here:

> *I see myself as a member of my group all the time and I have to really be careful with my words and deeds because others see me as their representative.*

—Shirley, Teacher, Chinese-English dual language program

As the discussion of collectivistic cultures in Chapter 1 emphasized, individuals in collectivistic cultures focus on cultivating and deepening relationships rather than on individual desires and actions, and becoming independent.

In Mexican, Dominican, Haitian, Somali, Chinese, and Hmong cultures, among others, meaningful interpersonal relationships are central (Falicov, 1998; Levine et al., 1994). For SLIFE who come from such collectivistic cultures, a key condition for learning is **interconnectedness** because the cornerstone of learning for most SLIFE is the unity of people and knowledge. Learning for SLIFE from collectivistic cultures is preferably interpersonal since they are generally accustomed to learning directly from another person whom one already knows and with whom one has an established relationship. Even in collectivistic cultures characterized by strong status differentiations, where teachers are viewed as authority figures, SLIFE often expect to have social relationships with their teachers. These relationships may entail knowing personal information about their teachers, and they may ask questions U.S. teachers consider inappropriate for the teacher-student roles in formal educational settings (Koch, 2007). Questions like "How many children do you have?" or "Why don't you live with your family?" are not construed by SLIFE as intrusive because they perceive this information as important. Questions such as these reflect the collectivistic orientation of many SLIFE for whom family and familial relations are fundamental, and one's identity cannot be separated from them (Tyler et al., 2008).

From the earliest school years, U.S. teachers encourage students to question and explore on their own, including questioning and challenging others' opinions, findings, and viewpoints. Students who come from cultures where authority is not questioned find such behavior threatening to the expected student-teacher social relationship (Jegede, 1994). As one American teacher commented:

> *When I make a mistake or offer a biased opinion unapologetically, a good student is not afraid to bring it up and call me on it. I like these types of students even if it means I lose a bit of face. It shows courage, independence, and leadership abilities.*

—John, high school social studies teacher

SLIFE may feel comfortable asking questions of their teachers that U.S. teachers find personal, private, and inappropriate. Yet, while they may expect to have greater personal knowledge than expected among U.S. teachers, many SLIFE adhere to strong notions of respect for and deferential behavior to the teacher, who represents authority and knowledge (Greenfield, Quiroz, & Raeff, 2000; K.H. Kim, 2005). Thus SLIFE, used to respecting the status of teachers, may find the questioning of authority inappropriate and uncomfortable.

Interconnectedness is fostered by regular student-to-student interaction, such that each student needs to feel connected to the others in the room and needs to be provided with many opportunities to develop and deepen the connections during the school day. Students who do not feel connected disengage (Suárez-Orozco, Suárez-Orozco, & Todorova, 2008). In the younger grades in U.S. classrooms, this type of interaction is built into the day, beginning with such common activities as Show and Tell or the recounting of personal experiences during share time. In secondary school, such interaction is expected to occur primarily outside of the classroom, during breaks, lunch, or after school. For SLIFE, social relationships need to be developed inside the classroom to lessen their sense of cultural dissonance and to help them develop a comfort level with the school.

In place of an interpersonal orientation, the U.S. system fosters a gradual separation of people and knowledge. While there are U.S. teachers who establish and maintain strong relationships with their students, the primary emphasis of these relationships is to support future independence (Althen, 2002). In place of an interconnected network of students and teacher that becomes stronger over time, the U.S. educational system moves in the opposite direction, to separate learners into individual islands of knowledge. The goal of K–12 instruction is for students not to "need" each other or the teacher, but rather to be successful learners on their own. Over the course of 12 years of schooling, students are expected to depend less on each other and less on their teacher. Beginning in pre-school, where the teacher is almost a parent, the student and teacher slowly become more distant until in college, professors do not necessarily know all the students. At that point, the focus is on the information, not the relationship between student and teacher. Popular strategies such as differentiated instruction focus on the individual needs, preferences, and abilities of students, with the goal of helping them reach their potential by making them responsible for their learning (Tomlinson, 1999). Although group work may be an important element in differentiated instruction, it is not seen as a *condition* for learning, but rather as a *support* for learning. Think about how this quote describes the frustration of one teacher:

"It's Like Pulling Teeth"

No matter what I say or what I do, Han and Guozhi never raise their hands, never look at me, and don't like to participate in any class activity unless it's small group work.
—*Mrs. Baldini*

1. **Based on the discussion of conditions for learning, what may be happening in Mrs. Baldini's classroom?**

2. **In what ways are Mrs. Baldini's assumptions about learning keeping her from understanding her students better?**

Component B: Processes for Learning in the Two Settings

Component B, processes for learning, focuses on how learning is conducted and transmitted. The two major processes SLIFE are accustomed to in negotiating the learning of new knowledge are (1) the sharing of responsibility among a group of learners who rely on one another and (2) taking in information and ideas in an oral, interactive mode (see Table 2.2). These two processes, **shared responsibility** and **oral transmission**, contrast directly with the processes SLIFE find in U.S. classrooms: individual accountability and print. Students in the U.S. are individually accountable for their own achievement, and, while the school and the classroom may be viewed as their own communities, the focus remains on the needs, abilities, and achievements of individual students (Alexander, 2000). Additionally, in the educational system, the primary vehicle for accessing and disseminating information is print. As students move through the grades, curriculum increasingly centers on literacy, so that by the time students are in high school, the expectation is that their learning primarily takes place through a reliance on their skills in deriving meaning from print.

Shared Responsibility versus Individual Accountability

Because SLIFE see themselves as being connected to one another as a group of learners rather than as independent learners, it follows that they prefer to learn together. SLIFE generally are not striving to distinguish themselves individually, but instead they tend to prefer to rely on each other and on their relationships to share their knowledge and understanding. To illustrate, in a Haitian bilingual program for SLIFE, the students spent mornings with their Haitian Creole teacher, Mrs. Rancey. The students and Mrs. Rancey worked through subject area content together in their native language with no individual or small group activities, nor was it a teacher-centered class. The class and Mrs. Rancey formed a single cohesive group. Through this interconnectedness, a sense of shared responsibility naturally developed in this classroom. This perspective directly contrasts with the Western-style formal educational model in which learners seek to show their independence and accept the fact that they will then be individually accountable for their own learning.

TABLE 2.2
Component B: Processes for Learning

SLIFE	U.S. Schools
Shared responsibility	Individual accountability
Oral transmission	Written word

This activity asks readers to consider different perspectives.

Board Work

Maria stands staring at the board in front of the class and struggles to solve the problem assigned to her by the teacher. Fellow students chime in with suggestions and guidance of all kinds. With their assistance, she is able to complete the problem successfully. Nevertheless, the teacher is disappointed and tells her that it would be so much better if she could do this all by herself without anyone's help.

1. Explain the students' perspective and the teacher's.
2. Consider what it means to share responsibility and what it means to be individually accountable from the perspective of the SLIFE and the U.S. teacher.

Readers may wish to point out that there is shared learning in U.S. classrooms— that is, cooperative learning. However, as pointed out in Chapter 1, cultural norms influence how people view collaboration and how they participate in cooperative learning activities (Siegler & Alibali, 2004). In U.S. classrooms that incorporate cooperative learning, groups do form and learn cooperatively; however, each student is ultimately given a specific job and must be accountable for it (Cohen, 1994). Take, for example, the popular cooperative activity, jigsaw (Aronson, 1978). In this activity, each member of the group is assigned one part of a learning task or problem and becomes an "expert" in that area. In larger classes, group members join with members of other groups with the same assignment to research and/or share ideas. After students have worked on their assignments, they rejoin their original groups to present their findings and to "piece together" a clear understanding of the learning task or problem. Each person's piece of the puzzle combines to form a completed jigsaw of knowledge; the students must rely on each other's expertise to obtain the necessary information to complete the group's learning task or problem. While there is group learning and group responsibility in the jigsaw activity, "students then apply their knowledge to a group task or to an individual task, assuring individual accountability for all information" (Peregoy & Boyle, 2008, p. 92).

As demonstrated and illustrated by the jigsaw activity, in the United States, group work is conducted as a team with each member responsible and accountable for a particular task or assignment to complete. For people of collectivistic cultures who have had minimal exposure to Western-style schooling, group work is enacted more as an ensemble (Mejia-Arauz et al., 2007). By extension, most SLIFE view learning as something that is accomplished cooperatively. The knowledge load is shared; they see themselves as a group of learners working together to construct knowledge. If we think of an orchestra, we think of the many players and instruments playing different notes, entering and ending at different times, yet the contributions of all the players playing together is what creates the music.

Different understandings and interpretations of the role of interconnectedness, shared responsibility, cooperation, and collaboration between U.S. schools and the previous experiences of most SLIFE are factors in the cultural dissonance experienced by them.

Oral Transmission versus the Written Word

Literacy is one of the primary criteria by which SLIFE are defined—that is, learners are evaluated based on their degree of literacy in either their native language or in English. In terms of the learning paradigm perspective we are using, literacy is a process for learning. Just as SLIFE bring with them a familiarity and comfort with learning through sharing knowledge, they bring a strong tradition of learning through oral transmission.

Some SLIFE come from cultures with little or no written language; others come from cultures with strong written traditions but have not had opportunities to develop strong literacy skills in their native language. This is a major difference within SLIFE. One further distinction among the groups of individuals who rely on oral language and other modes of communication, both verbal and nonverbal, rather than print, is whether they are subjected to self-esteem issues related to this. Many of the languages in the world have no written form, or have only recently developed one. These languages include many of the indigenous languages of peoples of Asia, Africa, and the Americas. Since literacy has not been embedded in these cultures or subcultures, there is often no stigma attached to those who do not obtain meaning from print. Knowledge, history, stories, and religious and cultural practices are all preserved and transmitted orally. Members of the culture who are most revered may not practice literacy at all (Shuter, 1985).

On the other hand, there are other cultures where literacy does play a major role, but many in the culture are disenfranchised from participating in education to develop literacy, usually a result of poverty and the lack of access to schools. In cultures where literacy is embedded in the majority culture, those members who do not have literacy are frequently stigmatized and face limited opportunities (Salomon & Apaza, 2006). Other SLIFE may be speakers of a language different from the majority language of their home country. The language they speak may not have a written form or may not be valued enough to be taught and/or may have few print materials. Such SLIFE have had unequal access to literacy since the majority language, which is generally also the language of schooling, is not their language. Because these students are generally not dominant in the majority language, they have been introduced to but have not mastered basic literacy skills, and therefore continue to face significant literacy issues (Commeyras & Inyega, 2007; Martin, 2008). Table 2.3, Typical Literacy Backgrounds of SLIFE, briefly summarizes variations of literacy SLIFE bring with them to the United States (see page 36).

All these SLIFE, share, however, a key perspective on literacy. They do not turn to print as a primary information resource for information or for developing their knowledge. As we saw in Chapter 1, print is not integral to their lives because typically their lives have not been centered on schooling. SLIFE often come from communities where

TABLE 2.3
Typical Literacy Backgrounds of SLIFE

Preliterate	Students speak languages that have no written form or that have just begun to be written. This is true of many languages in Africa and indigenous languages in Latin America and Southeast Asia.
Nonliterate	Although the language is written and may have a strong literary tradition, these students have not had access to literacy instruction.
Limited literate or semiliterate	Students have had some basic literacy instruction, but their literacy skills are significantly below the grade-level literacy expectations of the U.S. classroom.

there is little literacy, and print fulfills a minor, decontextualized role, generally limited to official and/or legal purposes. Literacy, if it even exists for their cultural group, is often restricted to a few adults, usually males, who function as de facto scribes for others (Whitescarver & Kalman, 2009).

SLIFE have had different life and school experiences. Literacy has not played an important role in their lives, nor have their prior literacy practices encouraged them to construct knowledge from print. SLIFE with basic literacy skills frequently view literacy as utilitarian. For instance, literacy can serve very specific and limited roles, such as reading the menu at McDonald's, looking at advertising flyers, or reading utility bills (Commeyras & Inyega, 2007; Lynch, 2009). When print is used, it must be contextualized and meaningful. It must be "brought to life" through extensive discussions among the reader(s) and the audience, which contextualize the impersonal text by supplying extensive background, for example, a description of how a particular dispute started, an examination of how the members involved are related, or the recounting of stories perhaps only tangentially related to the text (Salomon & Apaza, 2009). The text is secondary to oral communication.

Even storytelling, found in all cultures, is notably different between oral and written modes, demonstrating clearly the difference in conventions between oral and print. Print-based narrative storytelling uses a literary register without sustained efforts to "mimic orality through diction, syntax, or other devices of linguistic discourse" (Fugandes, 2007, p.138). Such narrative storytelling contrasts with oral storytelling, which uses and mimics the actual speech of characters by including representative syntax, accent, and vocabulary that "point to the world of primary orality" (p. 138). Oral transmission requires redundancy and repetition, or *backlooping*, and poetic devices used to facilitate memorization, such as redundancy and repetition of certain structures, provide rhythm and make it easier to remember. Instead of moving forward in each sentence as we do in written work, some of the same material is given again in the next sentence. We find this style in Homer and in early versions of the Bible, for example.

And God said: Be light made. And light was made. And God saw the light that it was good; and he divided the light from the darkness. (cited in Ong, 1982, p. 37)

U.S. schooling is based on the assumption that students will engage in continual, print-based textual interaction with content-area knowledge. A parallel assumption is that the print and the type of textual engagement increase in complexity as students progress through the grades. From the earliest grades onward, teachers and students together build meaning from print and create meaning with print. Children learn that reading and writing are interactive processes, where readers and writers consider what meaning is and how meaning is conveyed (Joyce, Weil, & Calhoun, 2009). As they develop their reading skills, children also develop important metacognitive skills such as monitoring, checking, and amending their reading processes (Gunning, 2008). In learning to write, children learn to organize and express their ideas in a variety of ways by practicing creating their own texts—whether functional, creative, or other—for different audiences.

The educational system is based on an evolving dependence on the written word for the retention and mastery of subject matter. Based on the belief that literacy development begins early in life and is ongoing, U.S. educators and psychologists advocate implementing literacy practices, including reading to children, providing an environment rich in literacy materials and activities, and nurturing children's desire to read through the use of specific reading practices beginning early in childhood (Morrow, 2005). Through print, which includes the Internet, people have immediate access to infinitely more information than any one person could possibly retain.

Such a different perspective on literacy between U.S. schools and SLIFE is another factor leading to the sense of cultural dissonance on the part of SLIFE. These students have difficulty making the transition from oral transmission to access of information from print, for example, in following directions from textbooks and using books to learn. These students, even after they are able to read, often turn to someone else to explain meaning to them because they continue to experience difficulties extracting meaning from print.

Component C: Activities for Learning in the Two Settings

Finally, we come to the largest overall difference between SLIFE cultural learning and formal education—the activities required of the learner. Just as we have seen the contrast between the conditions and processes for learning, we now examine the mismatch between the types of activities SLIFE are used to doing and the types of activities U.S. teachers expect them to do. In both paradigms the learners engage in activities that further their knowledge and mastery of skills. However, the tasks entailed in those activities differ greatly for the two paradigms. *Activities,* as a learning paradigm component, is a general or broad term encompassing a variety of tasks that are performed by the learner. Cooking, childcare, fieldwork, and construction work are examples of the types of pragmatic activities familiar to many SLIFE. The **pragmatic tasks** they perform in service of these activities have utilitarian results. Because SLIFE have primarily experienced learning in the context of real-world activities, they are accustomed to executing the types of tasks that directly result in the successful performance of those activities. Making soup, for example, is a pragmatic activity that entails such tasks as peeling vegetables, slicing them, and adding water. The end result will be a meal that satisfies a practical need for nourishment.

In contrast, Western-style education demands that SLIFE perform activities with tasks that do not have the same type of outcomes as pragmatic tasks. In the classroom, SLIFE must engage in a variety of academic activities with tasks that require that they think, talk, and write about what they are doing and why they are doing it (see Table 2.4). Students perform these tasks to demonstrate and further refine what is known as **academic ways of thinking**. Thus, for example, the activity of reading a story is developed through academic tasks, such as identifying the story elements and interpreting the significance of the narrative. The next section explores in detail how pragmatic and academic tasks differ and how academic ways of thinking manifest themselves in U.S. classrooms.

Pragmatic versus Academic Tasks

As discussed, SLIFE generally learn by doing, following a role model, operating within a context, and obtaining feedback from the results themselves or from people (Bassey, 1999). The key activity is practice, preceded by observation and followed by monitoring. Oral traditions continue to be important in transmitting knowledge and skills from adults to children in places that lack educational facilities and resources (Ishengoma 2005; Rogoff, 2003). Generally speaking, pragmatic activities occur within a context and have some real-world application that is immediately apparent. What we are referring to as academic activities, on the other hand, are activities that are designed for the purpose of analyzing and applying concepts that are generally presented with no real-world context.

In general, U.S. schools employ analytical activities, such as defining, categorizing and classifying, and synthesizing, to develop understanding by students. These academic ways of thinking underlie many of the learning activities conducted in U.S. classrooms. Memorization and rote learning have little place in schools today, yet they are often major strengths SLIFE bring with them as a result of their experiences with oral transmission. This strength gets them only so far, as the focus on academic activities forces them to use their knowledge in service of critical thinking rather than to accomplish a real-world task. For example, in social studies/history courses, students are asked to define terms and to analyze and interpret primary and secondary sources; in math they are expected to make logical deductions; in English they relate themes in literature to life and are expected to identify and explain different genres; and in science they must know the scientific method. These activities are neither intrinsically natural nor necessary for learning, but they are the way people are expected to learn

TABLE 2.4
Component C: Activities for Learning

SLIFE	U.S. Schools
Pragmatic tasks	Academic tasks

in formal educational settings. Bloom (1956) developed a taxonomy of academic ways of thinking and organized them into a hierarchy based on complexity. He associated them with classroom tasks and indicated how, taken together, the elements of the taxonomy could serve as a guide to the types of thinking required for a successful formal education experience. Chapter 6, which focuses specifically on this aspect of the learning paradigm, refers to Bloom's Taxonomy and its subsequent revised version (Anderson et al., 2001) as related to classroom projects for SLIFE.

Decontextualization

What makes academic activities so difficult for SLIFE is that they largely consist of decontextualized tasks, a key factor distinguishing the learning SLIFE are accustomed to from that of formal Western-style schooling (Ventura et al., 2008). We define *decontextualization* as "the handling of information in a way that either disconnects other information or backgrounds it" (Denny, 1991, p. 66). For those readers who may be familiar with Cummins' (1984) notion of context-reduced learning activities, it is important to underscore that we are using context differently. In Cummins' terms, *context-reduced* refers to the absence of *nonlinguistic* input devices, such as actions, gestures, drawings, multimedia presentations, and the like. *Context-embedded*, on the other hand, provides not only language, but also visual representations of that language or other types of enhancements that aid comprehension. In using the term *decontextualized*, however, we are referring to the absence of a real-world situation in which to place the learning activity. Although Cummins' point about context-reduced activities also applies to SLIFE, another issue relating to cultural factors for SLIFE is how information is presented. Specifically, how is academic knowledge separate from pragmatic knowledge?

In Chapter 1, for instance, we saw the question, "What do dogs and rabbits have in common?" We noted how this question would be answered differently, depending on a person's degree of participation in formal Western-style schooling.

Luria (1976) investigated preliterate farmers in a region of the former Soviet Union who had not been exposed to Western-style education. He showed the farmers four pictures: an ax, a hammer, a log, and a saw, and asked them to pick the one item they thought did not belong with the others. In this research, which has subsequently been replicated by many others across the world, Luria found that these farmers uniformly discarded one of the tools, usually the hammer, because for them, only the log provided a meaningful context, that of using the remaining tools to do something concrete with the log. Most people with Western-style education, in contrast, discard the log because the hammer, ax, and saw can all be categorized as tools. As shown in Chapter 1, categorization, based on abstract concepts, is an essential feature of Western-style education.

As we conclude this section on activities for learning, we note that SLIFE face a major challenge in learning not only how to perform academic tasks, but how to change the way they think about the world in order to reposition themselves to succeed with such tasks.

Two Contrasting Learning Paradigms

Table 2.5 summarizes the three components of a learning paradigm discussed in this chapter: Conditions for Learning, Processes for Learning, and Activities for Learning. For each, we see that the items on the left are in direct contrast to those on the right.

Because SLIFE have had limited or no exposure to Western-style education, they have a limited conceptual understanding of the U.S. learning paradigm. Their paradigm and ours conflict with each other, another factor in creating the sense of cultural dissonance experienced by SLIFE. Instead of immediate relevance and interconnectedness, SLIFE find that U.S. schools are future-oriented and promote independent learning. In place of their familiar processes for learning of shared responsibility and oral transmission, SLIFE are confronted with the expectation of individual accountability and learning primarily from print. Finally, SLIFE, who are accustomed to pragmatic tasks, encounter academic tasks and ways of thinking that do not match their experience.

TABLE 2.5
Two Different Learning Paradigms

SLIFE	U.S. Schools
Conditions for Learning	
Immediate relevance	Future relevance
Interconnectedness	Independence
Processes for Learning	
Shared responsibility	Individual accountability
Oral transmission	Written word
Activities for Learning	
Pragmatic tasks	Academic tasks

$\mathcal{F}$or Further Exploration

1. We all know how to work our own microwave, but when we encounter a different microwave, it takes a few minutes to figure out which buttons to push for which function. How can you relate this example to our initial discussion of formal schemata?

2. This vignette allows a glimpse into a SLIFE who faced major difficulties upon entering school in the United States and eventually dropped out.

   > Hayder, a Kurd refugee, entered high school with second grade literacy. He attended school but never completed homework assignments. However, outside of class Hayder "would read billboards while driving, signs on buildings, instructions and messages at an ATM, and messages and directions while playing video games" (Sarroub, Pernicek, & Sweeney, 2007, p. 676).

   a. How do you see this anecdote relating to the notion of immediate, practical relevance?

   b. How might Hayder's teachers have built on what he did like to read to motivate and engage him?

3. It could be argued that in mainstream U.S. culture, all of the elements on the left side of Table 2.5 not only exist but are embraced, and that it is only in school that the right side becomes the preferred paradigm.

   a. How does interconnectedness differ in a collectivistic culture from an individualistic one? If possible, provide examples.

   b. How can Americans see themselves as interconnected and yet focused on becoming independent? How does this relate to Question 3a?

4. Adnan is standing in the lab in front of his table looking at the directions for today's experiment. He reads carefully and then sits and waits for his teacher. His teacher is occupied across the room setting up the equipment for the final step in today's lab. She notices that Adnan has not begun his work. Based on the information in this chapter, what reasons can you suggest why Adnan may not yet have started working on his lab assignment? Consider, for instance, different assumptions about learning.

5. Mrs. Zukowski is working with her SLIFE class on the names of geometric shapes in English. After presenting the vocabulary to the students, she gives each student a bag that includes items with a variety of shapes, all in many different colors. She tells them to take these items out of the bag, sort them by shape, and then put all the squares, rectangles, etc., in the appropriately labeled boxes, which she has placed on a desk. When they are finished, she plans to review numbers by having the students count the number of items in

each box. After a few minutes, she realizes that the students aren't working on this activity and seem very confused. Initially, the teacher can't understand what the problem is; then she suddenly realizes that the SLIFE don't understand how they can group by shape if the shapes are different colors. For them, a red circle and a blue circle don't belong together, but a blue circle, blue triangle, and blue octagon do belong together. Based on the discussion in this chapter, how would you explain the difficulty SLIFE have focusing on shape and not color?

6. Mrs. Lehmann handed out a short survey to her ESL class asking them what they liked most and least about the class. For the question about what they liked the most, students answered: the vocabulary exercises, the discussion, the grammar work, and so on. The one SLIFE in the class responded instead, "I like that we all work together to help each other learn." In what way does this student's response parallel an element of the SLIFE learning paradigm?

3

An Introduction to MALP: The Mutually Adaptive Learning Paradigm

GIVEN THE MAJOR DIFFERENCES WE HAVE SEEN between the learning paradigm of SLIFE and the learning paradigm of U.S. schools, it is clear that what is needed is a type of bridge to assist this population in succeeding in our educational system. All too often, the general inflexibility of U.S. schools hinders the transition of students such as SLIFE to academic achievement and social integration (Koch, 2007; Nieto, 2004). On the one hand, a solution might be to teach SLIFE according to the conditions, processes, and activities of their own learning paradigm. In this way, they might feel more comfortable and more receptive to learning. However, ultimately, they cannot succeed in moving through the grades and in passing the standardized assessments with this approach. A second alternative is to teach according to the U.S. learning paradigm and expect SLIFE to catch onto it as they move through the system. Unfortunately, this plan also results in failure, as they cannot catch on and catch up due to the extreme cultural dissonance they are experiencing. The question then arises: what can teachers do? We argue that what is needed is a new instructional model that offers a mutually adaptive approach. Such an approach neither requires teachers to make a complete shift to the learner's paradigm nor tries to force students to make an immediate and complete shift to the U.S. learning paradigm. We have presented this instructional model previously (DeCapua & Marshall, 2010b; DeCapua, Smathers, & Tang, 2009; Marshall & DeCapua, 2010), but here we explore in depth what this model is and how it is implemented.

Addressing Cultural Dissonance

As a basis for proceeding, we need to consider how to address cultural dissonance. When teachers value their students' cultures and languages, they demonstrate an openness and willingness to accept differences. Teachers who know their students, their experiences, and their cultural backgrounds will be better able to utilize this knowledge to facilitate learning.

A focus on academic instruction by itself is not sufficient for SLIFE to become academically successful: the social nature of the classroom must be taken into account as well. A mutually adaptive instructional model does this by incorporating a socio-cultural perspective. From such a perspective, language, learning, and meaning are interconnected. The social practices and social nature of the classroom are as much a part of language learning as are understanding second language acquisition processes and being aware of current trends in second language teaching. Focusing exclusively or even primarily on the aspects of language that students must learn in order to develop proficiency, how students approach learning, and what teachers need to do to facilitate this learning is not enough. Theories of second language acquisition and good instructional strategies must be combined with an understanding of social contexts of language, learning, and meaning. Moreover, an effective classroom is a community, one with myriad interacting factors: social interaction; the beliefs, assumptions, and practices of students and teachers; the types of activities, their construction, and their implementation; and the nature of the relationships among the students and between the students and teacher. (See, e.g., Brown, 2003; DeCapua & Marshall, 2010a, 2010b; Hawkins, 2004; Marshall & DeCapua, 2010; Norton & Toohey, 2004.) This is the foundation of our mutually adaptive instructional model.

In this model, the teacher is not seen as the principle repository of knowledge but as one who learns with and from the students. Teachers learn from their students, identify with them as learners, and plan and revisit lessons accordingly. The role of the teacher is *both that of teacher and learner,* based on relationships and interactions deriving from this relationship. Methods and technical lesson delivery are not as important as interpersonal relationships with commitment, clear expectations, active engagement, and mutual respect because good teachers value their students and what they bring to the classroom (Clarke, 2006; Gay, 2000).

Teachers who have achieved notable success in challenging teaching situations do not adhere to one teaching philosophy and style of lesson delivery, and they often use several. However, what they all share is that they care about each and every child (Corbett, Wilson, & Williams, 2002). Because they have strong relationships with their students, these teachers are able to adapt their lessons and activities to meet the needs and abilities of each student, and they are sensitive to issues in their students' lives outside the classroom (Clarke, Davis, Rhodes, & Baker, 1996, cited in Clarke, 2006, p. 151). Although teaching methods are important, what is critical is how teachers deliver curriculum within the context of their classroom and with their students to create a positive learning environment (Patterson, Hale, & Stessman, 2007/2008).

The mutually adaptive model presented here is also informed by *culturally responsive pedagogy,* which holds that how teachers teach affects how students perceive the curriculum. Culturally responsive pedagogy focuses on teachers developing close relationships with their students and accommodating and responding to students' academic, cultural, linguistic, and social needs through their teaching approaches and strategies (Ladson-Billings, 1995). There have been extensive calls to make teachers more culturally responsive to their students—that is, to adapt their teaching to the way their students learn best (e.g., Gay, 2000; Villegas & Lucas, 2002). Nevertheless, there is evidence that pedagogy that adapts to the cultural patterns of the home and community does not necessarily help ELLs and/or SLIFE achieve academic success.

(See, e.g. Goldenberg, 2008; Nieto, 2010.) Such adaptations may make students feel more comfortable and accepted, leading to increased motivation, and, perhaps, greater accomplishment; however, this alone does not in and of itself produce school success in which students reach their potential academically. A mutually adaptive approach accepts the conditions shown to be most important for ELLs, particularly SLIFE (Component A) and *transitions* them to how they need to learn in the U.S. by combining the processes from both paradigms of learning (Component B), while focusing on new learning activities that develop academic ways of thinking (Component C).

To create a classroom as community and take into consideration culturally responsive pedagogy while transitioning SLIFE to the U.S. learning paradigm, we propose three principles as the basis of our instructional model, the Mutually Adaptive Learning Paradigm (MALP). This is a unified way to incorporate these principles insofar as they apply to SLIFE.

Principles for Addressing Cultural Dissonance in the SLIFE Classroom
1. Establish and maintain ongoing two-way communication.
2. Identify priorities in both cultures and accommodate where possible.
3. Build associations between the familiar and unfamiliar when accommodation is not feasible and new priorities must be established.

Establish and Maintain Communication

Too often schools set up one-way communication in which the role of the school is to inform students and their families, such as when schools translate materials and have meetings with an interpreter present. Although these initiatives are an important part of the school-family relationship, they are focused on conveying information, not necessarily on obtaining it. Communication however, should also flow in the other direction, so that school staff and teachers can listen to and learn from the families (Gehrke, 1998). It is true that some parents resist communication with the school, yet they may be more willing to share information and viewpoints if they are approached in a warm and friendly manner and with general rather than specific questions. SLIFE and their families have a great deal of information to impart to the school personnel about their background, their needs, their perspectives, and how they view the school experience (Delgado-Gaitan 2004; González, Moll, & Amanti, 2005). This knowledge will help classroom teachers to understand their students better and not simply see them as SLIFE, but as individuals who have outside responsibilities, such as having a job, taking care of younger siblings, or living alone as heads of household (Koch, 2007).

When communication occurs in both directions, there is more of an opportunity to reduce cultural dissonance for SLIFE and families new to the country. Once such communication has been established, teachers can obtain a great deal of knowledge that will assist in following the remaining two principles: identifying and accommodating priorities and making associations between familiar and unfamiliar concepts.

The scene described in the box, from Lewis Carroll's *Alice in Wonderland*, illustrates the importance of this first principle.

Explain Yourself

In *Alice's Adventures in Wonderland,* Alice encounters a very strange and peculiar world where animals and playing cards talk. After an incident in which Alice shrinks to a very small size and is wandering around among blades of grass, she encounters a mushroom about her height with a caterpillar sitting on top. When the caterpillar notices Alice, he asks, "Who are YOU?" and wants Alice to explain herself to him. She tells him that this is rather difficult because when she got up this morning she knew who she was, yet all manner of strange events have been happening to her and she is now rather confused as to who she is. Alice tries to explain her confusion to the caterpillar, who finds Alice's confusion strange and asks her again to explain who she is. Yet, when Alice asks the caterpillar who *he* is, he asks her why he should explain who he is.

1. How does this excerpt relate to the cultural dissonance addressed in this text? Consider how Alice's sense of reality has changed.

2. Explain how you can relate this excerpt to the idea of needing to establish and maintain communication with SLIFE.

FIGURE 3.1   Alice and the Caterpillar

Identify Priorities

The second principle is that of identifying priorities. People are generally unaware of their own cultural priorities because they are part of the subconscious knowledge members of a culture have by virtue of membership. As examined in Chapters 1 and 2, teachers and mainstream students in the U.S. educational system share a set of assumptions that can be seen as priorities for school. School priorities consist of that which is of most importance to teachers and/or students and that which must be in place for a successful teaching or learning experience. For example, in U.S. classrooms, it is understood and expected that all students are individually responsible for home-work assignments unless the teacher specifically says they can complete the work with others. This is a priority because it provides teachers with essential information on each student's grasp of the material, so that ultimately each student can receive the best instruction and a fair assessment in the form of a grade. SLIFE also have their own assumptions about learning that exemplify their cultural priorities. SLIFE generally believe that feelings of interconnectedness with fellow students and with the teacher are more important than being independent learners. Working together to share responsibility is a priority because it fosters their sense of community and helps to recreate their familiar learning paradigm.

Cultural dissonance is exacerbated when these assumptions are not brought to the level of awareness and dealt with in a culturally responsive manner. To address this principle, teachers must continually differentiate between what is important and what is a minor detail in each and every situation. This may seem like an obvious teaching strategy, since much of teaching focuses on identifying and conveying that which is important. The difference, however, is that teachers of SLIFE cannot lose sight of the fact that these students come, for the most part, from cultures with different learning paradigms and different formal schemata. What may be important within the context of the U.S. educational system may be very different from that which is regarded as important in the student's culture. In Latino cultures, for instance, *respeto,* or respect, is highly valued and considered an essential part of education (De Jesús &. Antrop-González, 2006). Similarly, what SLIFE may consider important or essential information or of significance may be overlooked, ignored, or considered minor when viewed from the formal academic point of view. The key point here is that when a priority for SLIFE can be accommodated, even if it differs from the teacher's priorities, it should be. One example is the need for immediate relevance. If SLIFE feel they cannot learn unless they see a connection to their lives, then the teacher can accommodate that priority. Teachers can seek to include elements of students' pragmatic knowledge and bring in content that incorporates their life outside of school.

When SLIFE need to honor a new classroom priority coming from the teacher, they will need to adapt. Although most SLIFE do not share print as a priority, the teacher will insist that the development of strong literacy skills and the ability to use these skills to access information is a priority in this new classroom setting. While in the past SLIFE have learned through oral transmission, they will need to prioritize literacy skills in order to succeed in school.

This give and take will demonstrate a willingness on the part of the teacher to take into account learner priorities while at the same time ensuring that the priorities on which learner success hinges, such as individual accountability, literacy, and academic ways of thinking, are enforced. In order to be effective in introducing new priorities, the teacher will need to use the third guiding principle, making associations between the familiar and the unfamiliar.

Recall in Chapter 1 the activity No Pencils, No Books (see page 23). Remember that you were asked to imagine being at a professional development meeting where there was no access to print material of any type. As highly educated people with a strong reliance on literacy, consider what bridges between the familiar (print) and the unfamiliar (exclusive oral transmission) would help you cope in a situation like this.

Build Associations

The third principle asks for teachers to build associations between the familiar and the new. Activating prior knowledge is one of the most important strategies in helping all students learn. In working with SLIFE, teachers must keep in mind that although these students may lack academic knowledge, they come to the class with substantial world experiences. When teachers relate the knowledge and experiences of SLIFE to the curriculum content, they form a bridge between the familiar and unfamiliar material (Trumball, Rothstein-Fisch, Greenfield, & Quiroz, 2001). In studying U.S. history, the teacher can begin with an event that may be familiar to the students. For example, for a unit on the Civil War and slavery, students may be familiar with issues of war and/or slavery from their own country.

Taken together, these three principles—establish and maintain communication, identify priorities, and build associations—function to address the cultural dissonance of SLIFE to help their transition to the U.S. learning paradigm. Teachers who infuse these principles into the daily work of teaching and interacting with SLIFE and their families will be taking a major step toward improving the school experience of SLIFE and reducing their cultural dissonance.

The Mutually Adaptive Learning Paradigm

Now let's see how each principle is operationalized in the service of effective instruction for SLIFE. In MALP, a new learning paradigm is created by taking elements from the two paradigms examined in Chapter 2. MALP accepts what is most essential for SLIFE and incorporates it into the classroom while taking what is most essential from the U.S. learning paradigm and retaining that in the classroom. The result is a model calling for both groups to accommodate the key learning priorities of the other. In this way, SLIFE have a level of comfort from the familiar aspects of their own learning paradigm as they are introduced to the new priorities of the U.S. learning paradigm, thereby reducing the students' sense of cultural dissonance. The MALP instructional model rests on the three components of any learning paradigm that were discussed earlier.

In MALP, for Component A, teachers adapt as they **accept the conditions** from the SLIFE paradigm, immediate relevance and interconnectedness, because these conditions for learning are priorities for SLIFE. For Component B, teachers and students both adapt to **combine the processes** from the two paradigms: shared responsibility + individual responsibility and oral transmission + print. For Component C, SLIFE must adapt as they **focus on new activities** requiring the performance of academic tasks. See Figure 3.2.

Before embarking on an in-depth analysis of these components, we consider two programs that exemplify the model. We have found that successful programs for this population often contain, without explicitly identifying them, elements of MALP. In particular, the following two studies highlight teachers and/or programs that are consistent with MALP and that have had positive results with SLIFE: The Haitian Literacy Program at Hyde Park High School in Boston (Walsh, 1999), the Bridging Cultures Project for Latino students in the Greater Los Angeles area (Rothstein-Fisch et al., 2003). Both demonstrate that SLIFE can be reached and can succeed with an approach that is mutually adaptive and attentive to the underlying aspects of culture.

Walsh (1999) describes in detail how the teacher in the Hyde Park program interacts with and teaches SLIFE, noting such factors as relevance, relationships, connecting oral and print modes, introducing individualistic aspects to students who are more comfortable relying on each other, and, ultimately, focusing on new activities required for success. Many students in this program not only learned to read and write but went on to graduate from high school, and some even attended college.

Rothstein-Fisch et al. (2003) discuss the successful engagement of young Latino students from eight elementary schools in the greater Los Angeles area in the Bridging Cultures Project. Although the particular project focused on elementary school students, rather than secondary-level students, their families had limited formal education, and the philosophy of the project closely parallels that of MALP.

The teachers in these programs all recognized that SLIFE have their own learning paradigm, one that is different but not deficient. As we look at each of the components

FIGURE 3.2   Mutually Adaptive Learning Paradigm

Adaptation	SLIFE Paradigm		U.S. School Paradigm
U.S. teachers adapt to SLIFE conditions for learning	**Immediate relevance** **Interconnectedness**		
SLIFE and U.S. teachers adapt to processes for learning from both paradigms	**Shared responsibility** **Oral transmission**	**+** **+**	**Individual accountability** **Printed word**
SLIFE adapt to U.S. classroom activities for learning			**Academic tasks**

of MALP in detail, readers should think about how programs they are familiar with may already incorporate some elements of this model.

Component A: Teachers Accept Students' Conditions for Learning

First, teachers must accept the conditions for learning from the learning paradigm of SLIFE: **immediate relevance** and **interconnectednes**s. MALP takes as a starting point these conditions as priorities of SLIFE: Teachers adapt their instruction in classes for SLIFE to accommodate the two conditions. As these two priorities are conditions that make SLIFE feel able and ready to learn, it behooves teachers to design instruction and create classroom communities in such a way as to honor these conditions. Moreover, by accepting their conditions for learning, teachers focus on interconnectedness, consistent with the principle of establishing and maintaining ongoing two-way communication with SLIFE. The condition of interconnectedness also includes instruction that promotes connections among students as well. Finally, by accepting immediate relevance, teachers focus on incorporating familiar material into their lessons, making associations between past experiences and current life situations of SLIFE and the new material teachers are teaching.

Ensuring Immediate Relevance

In Chapter 2, we introduced the idea that the way in which relevance is construed in the U.S. educational system is different from the understanding many SLIFE have of relevance. Relevance in MALP means making connections between the pragmatic worldview of SLIFE and the academic world of schooling; it means making learning relevant to the here and now, rather than to some time in the future.

To incorporate immediate relevance, the teacher begins each unit of instruction with the ways in which the material can be incorporated into the lives of the students. Mary Jo, a high school social studies teacher, writes:

> At this point in the year the class is studying westward expansion, the idea of Manifest Destiny, and the conflicts involved (Mexican-American War, Native American conflicts) in this process. I decided to take the usual lessons regarding the Oregon trail and adjust them according to some of the principles I read about in the MALP articles. Following the ideals of MALP I knew that my lesson needed to be personal and immediately relevant. The easiest way to do this was to begin the lesson with a brief class discussion about why we move to new places, what motivates us to move, how we survive once we arrive. The students shared some very good stories, learning more about each other (building those social relationships) and also sharing some funny experiences they had when they arrived and had to communicate, shop for groceries, etc.

Mary Jo's lesson is not planned simply for motivation but also to give the students specific information and skills they can use. Learning parallels the changes in their lives. Nearly all of the curriculum can be viewed through this lens, but it must be a priority in lesson planning, rather than an afterthought. Once the stage is set in this way, SLIFE begin to regard education as something related to their lives.

Ensuring Interconnectedness

Interconnectedness is, as we saw in Chapter 1, a central tenet of collectivistic cultures, from which the majority of SLIFE come. Because group membership and group relationships are primary to students from such cultures, learning from and with each other, as well as the teacher, is important. Thus, interconnectedness is also a central tenet of MALP—interconnectedness with each other and with the teacher (Niyozov, 2008/2009).

To create an interconnected classroom community, teachers need to infuse instruction with interpersonal elements. Although many U.S. teachers, especially those teaching younger students, would feel that this is something any good teacher does, their understanding of "relationship" is not necessarily the same as that of SLIFE. In the United States, Americans tend to compartmentalize their lives and relationships into work, school, family, and so on. Teachers generally do not expect or want students to visit them unexpectedly or to be invited (or expected to attend) important family celebrations of their students. Most U.S. teachers consider very personal questions from their students to be intrusive and rude.

In classrooms across the U.S., research has shown that the most effective teachers are those who take responsibility for both the affective and academic domains in the classroom—that is, teachers who are well organized, well able to present the requisite material to their students, and who have a strong relationship with their students (Cazden, 2001; Clarke, 2007; DeCapua, Smathers, & Tang, 2009; Ladson-Billings, 1995). Being a good teacher is not only about a search for the latest and best techniques and materials, but it is also about establishing genuine relationships with one's students. Good techniques and materials are important, but these are *tools* of teacher-student relationships and not *ends in themselves* (italics added, Clarke, 2007, p. 131). For most SLIFE, moreover, these relationships are a key condition for them to learn. When SLIFE find themselves in classrooms that do not foster strong interconnectedness, they tend to feel alienated and isolated, increasing their cultural dissonance. If teachers accept the long-term priority to connect, SLIFE are more likely to engage and to learn than if the teacher insists exclusively on independent learning in the very beginning.

Reforms intended to address student disengagement and dropout rates argue for the need to restructure high schools to encourage interconnectedness among students and between students and teacher. Support for the first component of MALP, accept students' conditions for learning, is evident in the research. Schlosser (1992) found that while interconnectedness can benefit all students, it is particularly critical for students from a different learning paradigm than that of the U.S. Sarroub et al. (2007), in their case study of a struggling SLIFE, describe how one teacher especially made social connections with the student, often inquiring about personal topics such as his family or car problems. Such social connections are central to MALP. It is essential that teachers make it a priority to have students relate to one another in significant ways, as well as to the teacher. The following chapters will explore how activities and projects within the MALP framework provide opportunities for creating closer relationships.

Fostering a strong sense of interconnectedness may seem difficult because it requires time to develop student-to-student and teacher-to-student relationships, especially in a high school setting where the subject matter often takes center stage and the structure of the school day with its discrete periods often precludes extended contact time. Nevertheless, with SLIFE, it is essential to make relationships a priority because, in the end, the students become invested in the learning when it is situated in an interconnected learning community created by the teacher, as this vignette illustrates:

Teacher-to-Student Relationship

Phong, a 17-year-old SLIFE from Vietnam, was not a particularly committed student. One day, he came to see Mrs. Higgins in her classroom after school. He spent about an hour asking Mrs. Higgins questions about her work life, her home life, and her general outlook on life as a whole and then left. Mrs. Higgins felt bewildered. She had expected that eventually Phong would come to the point of why he had requested the meeting, perhaps for extra help or to discuss some problem he was having related to school.

The next day in class, Phong was a different student. He was engaged in the lesson, smiled, and was interested in learning the new material. After class, Mrs. Higgins asked him about the change in his behavior and he explained, "Now I know you, I can learn from you."

1. **Explain what led to the change in Phong's outlook.**

2. **How does this relate to the concept of interconnectedness?**

3. **How does this concept differ from behaviors in mainstream U.S. schools?**

When the conditions are in place in the classroom, SLIFE can cope with the challenges of learning English and content knowledge, developing literacy skills, and developing academic ways of thinking. Teachers who incorporate and foster the two major conditions SLIFE want and need find that they do not need to sacrifice the goals and objectives of English language and subject area content mastery. With the affective factors addressed—the conditions for learning—SLIFE can turn more constructively to the academic factors. Because they can find what they seek in terms of their relationships in the classroom and the face validity (i.e., immediate relevance) of the material they are learning, they are more likely to take the extra step to learn new material and try new learning strategies (DeCapua & Marshall, 2010b; Marshall, DeCapua, & Antolini, 2010).

In order to be receptive to accepting the conditions for learning of SLIFE, teachers need to infuse their lessons with opportunities for fostering interconnectedness and making learning relevant in a new way.

Component B: Students and Teachers Combine Processes for Learning from Both Paradigms

The second component of MALP is to combine the processes for learning. By combining, we mean that teachers incorporate the processes that SLIFE normally use—**shared responsibility** and **oral transmission**—into their lessons with the processes SLIFE must master to achieve in U.S. schools, namely **individual accountability** and the **printed word.** Teachers combine the processes for learning to assist SLIFE in their transition from the familiar to the unfamiliar. By careful infusion of the MALP model into their instruction, teachers create bridges between shared responsibility and individual accountability and between oral transmission and the written word. In using MALP, teachers accept the importance of sharing with peers and the oral mode of passing along new information. They understand how new and even threatening individual accountability may be for SLIFE and how alien and disorienting learning from print may be.

Moving from Shared Responsibility to Individual Accountability

In implementing MALP, teachers consistently combine the familiar process of shared responsibility with the new one of individual accountability. A MALP classroom incorporates much more cooperative work than a traditional secondary classroom. While the cooperative classroom is encouraged and indeed viewed as central to good teaching, especially in the elementary grades (see, e.g., Joyce, Weil, & Calhoun, 2009), far too often teachers continue to teach traditionally; this is even more so as students move up through the grades (Abrami, Poulsen, & Chambers, 2004; Siegel, 2005). Allowing and encouraging SLIFE to share and learn informally from each other and from the teacher fosters the sense of the classroom as a community. Conversational interaction is the first priority. Teachers need to ensure, however, that students remain on task when engaging in cooperative learning. They further need to be aware that students' attention may wander or be distracted by material that is too difficult and is not adequately scaffolded.

When teachers introduce a task requiring individual accountability in a lesson or activity, it is essential that they identify specifically what students are to complete on their own. This should be modeled first, step-by-step, so that the SLIFE see exactly what is expected of them. Initially, tasks requiring individual accountability should be short, to give SLIFE an opportunity to become accustomed to working alone. As SLIFE become more comfortable with individual work, these tasks can become longer and more involved.

Moving from Oral Transmission to the Written Word

SLIFE have different needs from high school ELLs with a literacy and education background, necessitating different methods and approaches to literacy. As older adolescents with few or no literacy skills, they may suffer psychological barriers in developing these skills, such as frustration, anxiety, and low self-esteem, and, in the case of refugee students, war trauma (Magro, 2008). In terms of the new experiences with literacy SLIFE are encountering, work on adult literacy informs our understanding of how to introduce and develop literacy among older students (see, e.g., Kruidenier, 2002). The Brazilian educational philosopher Paolo Freire, for example, has argued that when literacy functions as a social awakening and empowering action, developing literacy skills becomes meaningful to adult students. If SLIFE can come to see literacy as a powerful tool that can change their lives in a meaningful way and not only as a requirement of an unfamiliar and alien school system, they become engaged more in mastering literacy skills (DeCapua & Marshall, 2010b; Marshall, DeCapua, & Antolini, 2010). For literacy to be meaningful to adult students, it must be built around their needs, interests, and daily lives (Freire, 1994; Kagitçibasi, Goksen, & Gulgoz, 2005).

An essential process of MALP is to transition SLIFE to the primacy of literacy in the U.S. learning paradigm by combining oral transmission and the written word. In so doing, teachers scaffold transition to print by building on the strength of SLIFE, oral communication. It is important to emphasize, as discussed in Chapter 2, that including activities that use oral transmission is not simply making oral language integral to completing activities in the classroom. Oral transmission goes beyond reciting, repeating, or even talking; it refers to the act of conveying information and knowledge to hearers. It entails a great deal of built-in redundancy to help hearers learn and retain the information being conveyed. For example, teachers incorporating oral transmission infuse their lessons with such devices as call and response questions: "What's the first step you need to do?" or "Now what are you going to have to do for this assignment?" Teachers need to provide such devices to deliver oral instruction effectively given that SLIFE are accustomed to oral language that embeds devices for retention.

Component C: Students Learn New Classroom Activities

For Component C, the final, and perhaps most critical component of MALP, students must learn how to engage in **new classroom activities** that develop academic ways of thinking. For SLIFE to master these academic ways of thinking, MALP asks teachers to focus on a variety of academic tasks, being sure to make them accessible by scaffolding them with familiar language and content. By having the conditions in place (Component A) and combining the processes (Component B), SLIFE can be introduced to and practice academic types of activities that lead to academic ways of thinking. Scaffolding these academic activities is central to the successful implementation of the MALP instructional model.

Learners understand new information within the context of what they already know, which is why it is difficult for all students, not just SLIFE, to understand abstract academic concepts and apply them to new tasks (Willingham, 2009). People are less likely to recall information that does not fit their schemata (Kee & Davies, 1990). For SLIFE, coming from a different learning paradigm with different schemata, academic ways of thinking are particularly difficult. Comparison/contrast, analysis, synthesis, and similar academic ways of thinking are integral to Western-style formal education. As mentioned in Chapter 2, Bloom's Taxonomy provides explicit descriptions of these ways of thinking and how they relate to classroom activities and can serve as a guide for teachers as they implement Component C of MALP.

A key to improving students' ability to understand the abstract thinking underlying academic activities is for them to do these new activities repeatedly with different information and within different contexts. It is through extended practice, as in the MALP instructional model, that SLIFE become proficient at academic ways of thinking. Critical-thinking skills, or academic ways of thinking, are closely tied to background knowledge (Echevarria, 2003; Willingham, 2007). Thus, it is critical that teachers of SLIFE help these students both acquire content knowledge and develop their academic or critical thinking skills, while at the same time developing academic language proficiency. The question is: How do teachers do this?

In order to understand the way MALP addresses this question, we return to schema theory, introduced in Chapter 2, and the opening activity in the chapter, which looked at the months of the year and how they are stored in the brain. We pointed out that a learning paradigm can be thought of as a cluster of schemata that people bring to the task of learning. Students bring to any learning activity three kinds of schemata: linguistic schemata, content schemata, and their formal learning schemata from their learning paradigm. To illustrate, consider these two very different activities for SLIFE:

Academic Ways of Thinking Using Familiar Language and Content

Classroom Activity 1: Tell a culturally traditional folktale in your language.
Classroom Activity 2: Write a science lab report in English.

a. Which activity uses familiar language?

b. Which one has familiar content?

c. Which one has familiar formal schemata?

d. Can you explain which activity is easier for SLIFE, using schemata theory as the basis for your explanation?

In Activity 1, all three schemata are familiar to SLIFE: The language is familiar because it is the native language; the content is familiar because it asks SLIFE to recount a folktale they know; and the formal schema is familiar as well because it is a story from the native culture and based on a rhetorical form familiar to SLIFE. This type of activity could be an opportunity for students to share with others and might be used in a bilingual program for native language arts development. However, such an activity by itself is not enough in MALP because it does not practice and develop the academic ways of thinking, as required for Component C.

In Activity 2, all three schemata are unfamiliar. First, the language is not only English, but academic English. Second, the content is new and relatively unfamiliar because it is based on a science experiment from this week's lesson. And, finally, the formal schema is unfamiliar because the SLIFE must write a lab report, which has very specific rhetorical organization and form.

The balancing of schemata requires that the new formal schema of the academic task be the primary unfamiliar aspect of the activity. Therefore, to help SLIFE learn the academic ways of thinking of Component C, teachers introduce only the formal learning schemata, while controlling that language and content are familiar, a practice valuable for native speakers and essential for SLIFE. A coin collector, for example, is more likely to be able to work out a problem on fractions if the problem is framed in terms of exchanging money than if the problem is framed in terms of calculating the efficiency of an engine because in the former the language and content are familiar (Willingham, 2009, p. 91). Building on this example, each academic learning activity teachers assign SLIFE should occur in the context of familiar linguistic and content schemata, allowing SLIFE to focus on academic ways of thinking without the added complications of unfamiliar language and content. While SLIFE certainly need to develop their language proficiency and subject matter knowledge, from the MALP perspective, linguistic and content learning are separate from learning academic ways of thinking.

To summarize, the MALP instructional model incorporates elements from both the learning paradigm of SLIFE and from the learning paradigm of U.S. schools, creating a third learning paradigm in which both sides adapt. In this way, neither the students nor the teachers must completely alter their approach to the classroom. By accepting the conditions of learning from the SLIFE learning paradigm, teachers adapt their instruction to accommodate the needs of their students. By teachers' explicit combining of key processes from both paradigms, SLIFE more easily make the transition to key processes of the U.S. paradigm, individual accountability and print. By scaffolding activities that introduce and practice academic ways of thinking, SLIFE learn to think academically, not only pragmatically.

MALP has, then, explicitly addressed the three principles for addressing cultural dissonance—maintaining two-way communication, identifying priorities, and building associations. The communication element is evident in Component A, for which the teacher establishes interconnectedness in the MALP classroom. The identification of priorities from both cultures is evident in the way in which MALP accommodates some priorities from the SLIFE learning paradigm while requiring SLIFE to adapt to key priorities from the U.S. teachers' paradigm—individual accountability, the written word, and academic tasks. In Component B teachers encourage the development of individual accountability and familiarity with print by associating them with the familiar processes for SLIFE—shared responsibility and oral transmission. In Component C, teachers introduce academic ways of thinking through academic learning activities based on familiar language and content to assist SLIFE in making associations, even as they develop new schemata. Finally, building associations between familiar and unfamiliar is clearly integral to both Components B and C. By creating a MALP classroom, teachers can maximize the opportunity for SLIFE to succeed in their new classroom setting. The MALP approach ensures that both teachers and students work together to create a classroom environment that is a positive, challenging, yet supporting setting for this population. Subsequent chapters explore more specifically how MALP is implemented in SLIFE classes.

*F*or Further Exploration

1. Getting to know each other and feeling a sense of interconnectedness is important for all students. Explain how this is even more important for SLIFE and why it might be more difficult or unusual at the secondary level than in earlier grades. Design some ways that you could increase your interconnectedness with your SLIFE. What might you do differently that would help them to feel connected to you and more able to learn from you?

2. Mrs. Biscoglio, presented with the notion of interconnectedness and MALP, feels it doesn't apply to her:

   > I'm already very close with my students. I believe that relationships are the key to learning and I already know that. This isn't a helpful concept for me as I already incorporate this condition into my classroom every day.

   a. Explain how interconnectedness as the SLIFE perceive it is different from relationships that all good teachers have with their students.

   b. Discuss how you might make the concept of interconnectedness clearer and more comprehensible to Mrs. Biscoglio and others like her.

   c. Discuss how interconnectedness is different from shared responsibility.

3. Take an activity that you already do and find a way to make it focus on the whole class as a group without dividing the class at all and without the activity being teacher directed. Do not assign roles but allow students to function as a group assisting each other.

4. Design an activity for students that requires them to create an oral version of something presented in print. Do the reverse as well. What do you notice is different in the two activities you are designing?

5. Ms. Lopez has the students work with a partner on a regular basis for part of each math lesson. However, even though each student has a partner, she allows them to consult with other students as well. She has trained them to guide each other and not give the answer—a skill they are proud of mastering. Because she has focused on teaching the steps of problem solving, they help each other with a given step and then let the other student work on that step. When the native language is used for this purpose, the teacher permits their speaking in that language and then asks them to use English when the class comes back together. Because some SLIFE are better at math and some are better at English, there is a great deal of sharing in Ms. Lopez's classroom. How does Ms. Lopez's approach reflect the MALP classroom? Explain your answer by referring to the components of MALP.

4

Infusing Lessons with MALP

THIS CHAPTER INTRODUCES READERS to the ways in which MALP can be infused into lessons. First, we discuss the importance of learning objectives and why they differ for SLIFE when implementing MALP-based lessons. We will see how two teachers, Christina and Rick, using content-based ESL instruction, incorporated MALP to make their instruction more effective for SLIFE. We will examine in detail Christina's three-day lesson sequence and how she included each element of MALP. We will also examine Rick's hands-on math lesson and how he used a checklist designed specifically for this approach.

An extremely important challenge for high school SLIFE is the need to attain grade-level performance academically at the same time they are struggling to master English, develop literacy skills, and adjust to school culture. To accomplish this, they must focus from the very beginning on developing academic English, in addition to everyday conversational skills, because academic English is the language of schooling. A way to facilitate academic language proficiency is to introduce language via the content rather than isolating English language and literacy skills, as through a content-based approach (Cantoni-Harvey, 1987; Echevarria, Vogt, & Short, 2008). In this approach, teachers incorporate content from different subject areas, often through thematic units or project-based learning (see Chapter 5). Content-based ESL instruction, when implemented in conjunction with MALP, is especially valuable for high school SLIFE since they have so few years to achieve content-knowledge parity with their peers.

Lesson Planning and Academic Task Objectives

Lesson planning using MALP is similar in many ways to planning lessons for any secondary school classroom. However, we recommend certain modifications to maximize the effectiveness of the lesson with SLIFE. One of these modifications affects the design of learning objectives. The Sheltered Instruction Observation Protocol, or SIOP®, an instructional model for ELLs, is widely recognized as valuable in delivering language and content to them. The originators of SIOP® have been instrumental in stressing the all-important link between language and content, advocating that both be included in all lessons prepared for classes having ELLs. As a result, many ESL and content area teachers now create both language and content objectives for their lessons. Readers are referred to the SIOP® materials for detailed discussion of the Lesson Preparation component of SIOP®, in which the developers of that model present instructions and examples for both types of learning objectives (e.g., Echevarria & Graves, 2007; Echevarria, Vogt, & Short, 2008).

These two types of learning objectives, language and content, are as essential for SLIFE as for other ELLs. However, for SLIFE, these two objectives are not sufficient for comprehensive lesson planning. We argue that there should be a third type of learning objective, an academic task objective. SLIFE, like all ELLs, need language and content. Developing academic language and building a foundation in the content knowledge expected of high school students are properly the focus of instruction. But, because they are SLIFE, they also need to develop the academic ways of thinking that most of their peers have been engaging in since the early grades.

Earlier chapters revealed that the formal schemata of school create the major barrier to success for SLIFE and that academic tasks exemplify these schemata most clearly. Although SLIFE are acquiring new language and content schemata, if the formal schemata used to teach the new language and content are unfamiliar, they will be unable to access the instruction in the way that other ELLs can. The formal schemata required in U.S. schooling should appear in the form of a learning objective along with the other two. The third component of MALP, Component C, calls for teachers to focus on tasks that introduce and practice academic ways of thinking. Because academic tasks are a key component of MALP, they must be explicitly stated as objectives on lesson plans for SLIFE. These academic tasks may be completely new, or may be a more complex version of an academic task already introduced and practiced. This task becomes the focus of the lesson or lessons over several days. The academic ways of thinking outlined and discussed in Chapters 2 and 3 underlie the academic task objectives. Table 4.1 provides some specific illustrations, accompanied by the tasks that exemplify them, and the learning objectives for this third schema, the formal schema that increases familiarity with and competence in performing academic tasks.

TABLE 4. 1
Academic Ways of Thinking

New Way of Thinking	Academic Task	Academic Task Objective
Distinguishing between or among items	Compare and contrast	Students will be able to identify similarities and differences between or among items
Grouping similar items	Classify or categorize	Students will be able to sort items into groups based on criteria provided
Establishing chronology	Sequence	Students will be able to place items in order of occurrence in time and/ or in a process

The process of designing instruction will differ for the individual teacher, the content area, the district curriculum, and the state standards. The next section shows how one teacher, Christina, who teaches ESL and social studies for SLIFE, infuses MALP into her lessons. She is cognizant of following the three components of MALP and ensuring that they are infused as a lesson progresses.

Social Studies Scenario

This week, Christina is teaching her self-contained SLIFE class about the presidential election. She has already worked with the SLIFE on the concept of individual voting as part of the democratic system and how that differs from a group reaching consensus, as some of the students are used to from their experience in their native countries. She is trying to convey the idea that it is the population of a state, not its physical size, that determines how many votes it is given to choose the president. The underlying concept is that of the Electoral College, a difficult concept even for many American students. To avoid getting into details but help them understand that there is an additional step that affects the outcome of the presidential election, Christina merely introduces the vocabulary *state*, *population*, and *states' votes*. Her goals are to follow the mandated social studies curriculum without overwhelming her students with too much information and to develop her students' academic ways of thinking, for example, comparison/contrast.

To have enough time for the students to engage in a culminating activity for this sequence of lessons, Christina uses double periods of ESL and social studies. For such an activity, a minimum of three to five periods is usually required.

Christina begins with her language and content objectives for this six-period, three-day, lesson sequence. In addition to her objectives for English language proficiency development and her objectives for social studies following MALP, Christina has an academic task objective: In each lesson, she will introduce or further develop academic ways of thinking through an unfamiliar task. Over the course of three days, she focuses on this task to ensure that the SLIFE become accustomed to this new way of thinking. Here is an overview of her three-day plan:

Christina's Three-Day Plan for Her Self-Contained SLIFE Class
Day 1: Building background about the election and the candidates
Day 2: Learning to use the Internet to find information on current events Collecting and recording data for two states
Day 3: Comparing and contrasting electoral votes for two states Creating and sharing a poster with the information

Christina prepares for the lesson sequence by finding websites about the election that are preselected for clarity, visuals, and minimal text. She also finds one or two websites in the native languages of her SLIFE whenever possible. She bookmarks these sites in a social bookmarking application (delicious.com or another such tool) with her name so that students will be able to search among the sites from her page. (See Chapter 7 for more about bookmarking.) Christina also prepares a poster to be used as a model for the ones that her students will complete as their culminating activity for these lessons.

Day 1

Christina asks her students to name any state they have heard of or have some connection to in their personal lives; the class then goes together to that state's website—to see pictures, to see the state on the map, and to learn something new about the state. The students and Christina discuss how the size of a state does not correlate with the number of people who live there. New Jersey, for instance, is much smaller than Montana, yet New Jersey has a much higher population. Once they have viewed several states on the Internet, Christina shows them a chart with the names of the states they have asked her about and two numbers: population and states' votes.

State	Population	State Votes
New York	19,490,297	31
Pennsylvania	12,448,279	21
California	36,756,666	55
Texas	24,326,974	34

Next, Christina asks the SLIFE if they know who is running for president in the upcoming election and if they know anything about the candidates. They talk and share ideas while Christina makes notes on chart paper with key words from the students' contributions. The SLIFE are allowed to use their native languages when they don't know the English words; they help each other say the words in English. After Christina has finished writing their notes, the students read them aloud together. They then practice forming sentences based on the notes. She has bookmarked some websites for them to browse when they go to the lab the next day and puts the notes the students made together up on the wall. These notes are designed to guide the students in finding out more on their own.

Day 2

Today this self-contained ESL social studies class for SLIFE meets in the computer lab. Christina gives each student a graphic organizer to complete. She asks them to work with a partner and gives each pair two different states to research. They find their states on Christina's bookmarking page and collect information about each state's population and number of votes, pictures of the state, the shape of the state, and the state's size in relation to other states as seen on a U.S. map that Christina has hung on a wall. To differentiate instruction for more advanced students, Christina suggests that they collect other information that they find interesting about the two states. After the SLIFE have had time to find information about their states, Christina asks each student to choose one of the two states and to collect any extra information the pair would like to have about their two states. Each pair prints out at least two photos and the shape of the state from the website.

Day 3

The students are back in their classroom. Christina shows them a completed poster, in which she has compared and contrasted two states. She tells them that they will produce a similar poster. She points to her poster as she explains each item: the title, the names of the states, the pictures, the shapes and sizes, the population figure, and the number of votes these states have. The bottom of Christina's poster includes a comparison/contrast sentence using *although*:

> **Although Wyoming is larger than Virginia, Virginia has more electoral votes because it has more people.**

After she finishes pointing to the different parts of her poster, she has each student come to her poster, point to an item on the poster, and explain what that item is. Yaneit wants very much to be first. She comes up, points to the picture of Virginia on the poster, and says, "This Virginia, I know, my aunt live there." Yaneit chooses to volunteer to be first because she can relate to one picture personally and wants to share this with the rest of the class.

Christina's comparison/contrast sentence at the bottom of the poster is not an easy one for the SLIFE. In order to help her students understand this sentence, Christina provides scaffolding, showing the SLIFE how each part of the sentence comes from the data on the poster by pointing to the sentence and the data as she reads. She elicits the data orally and asks one student to write each sentence on the board, based on sentence frames.

Sentence frames are mini-templates into which students insert the appropriate words (Nattinger & DeCarrico, 1992). Such frames allow students to see and produce accurate sentence patterns—that is, grammatically correct sentences—without becoming bogged down in grammar rules (Wood, 2002). While sentence frames have become an accepted best practice for ELLs (see, e.g., Carrier, 2005), these frames are especially important in scaffolding writing skills for SLIFE. Christina uses frames like the following as scaffolding for this lesson:

> *(name of state A)* has _____ people and _____ electoral votes.

While many ELLs may succeed even without such techniques, SLIFE most likely will not given that they need additional help in accessing academic ways of thinking.

After they have worked through the various statements, the students are ready to understand Christina's comparison/contrast statement about her two states: *Although Wyoming is larger than Virginia, Virginia has more electoral votes because it has more people.*

Once the students are comfortable with what Christina expects to see on their posters, each pair works on preparing a poster with visuals, data, and a comparison/contrast statement. When all the students have completed their posters, the pairs take turns presenting their posters to the rest of the class. Each person in the pair talks about one of the two states. The pair chooses another student in the class to read the final comparison/contrast statement they have written at the bottom of their poster.

Discussion of Christina's Lessons

We now look carefully at Christina's three lessons to see how she has infused the three components of MALP: A, accept the conditions; B, combine the processes; and C, focus on new activities. We also see how she applies the two elements of each component. Christina has incorporated one condition for learning, **immediate relevance**, from different perspectives: current events, geography, and cultural background, in addition to the social studies curriculum content. In this way, each student may find one or another perspective more compelling. As the topic is the election, those students who follow the news or hear about the news from others may become more enthusiastic about the activity. To bring them closer to the topic, Christina selects their own state, New York, as one of the states for modeling the activity.

Another strategy to make lessons more immediately relevant is to capitalize on the natural links across disciplines that are often ignored in secondary school classrooms. Because this lesson sequence involves numbers, Christina found ways to collaborate with the math teacher. In the math class, the SLIFE have been learning about rounding numbers so Christina asks the math teacher to use the population figures from the students' posters about the states as examples. In addition to showing SLIFE how what they are learning in one class may assist them with what is going on in another, this type of collaborative effort among teachers gives the students an opportunity to revisit and practice concepts. While making connections across content areas is important for all students, such redundancy and reinforcement is especially important for SLIFE.

Christina's lesson sequence contains many opportunities for her students to develop and maintain **interconnectedness** with her and with each other. Over the three days of this project, the SLIFE had personal connections to various states that came up in the Internet research. They were encouraged to select states with which they had some family connection. Claude wanted to explore Pennsylvania because he had an aunt there; Yolanda wanted to look at Arizona because her brother had been there. During this time, the students wanted to share their opinions about the presidential candidates, especially once they had begun the activity, and they looked for information about them at the sites Christina had bookmarked. In the process of exploring their chosen states and in discussing their opinions about the candidates, the students learned more about each other. As they worked with their partners in their Internet search and in creating their posters, the students had further opportunities to connect.

Christina has built in extensive partner work, which SLIFE find familiar and comfortable. The partner work in this activity extends across all three days, and the two students who are working together spend most of their time together, even in the lab where they sit at adjacent computers. Christina encourages them to **share the responsibility** and assist each other in finding the information they need. Together they look for the required information about their states, but each of them takes ownership for one state in writing the information on the graphic organizer. This **individual accountability** component is an enhancement to the main task, which is completed together. The poster is a joint effort, although each student will compose parts of it, and they work out together how it will look in terms of layout, content, text, and visuals. Finally, the oral presentation provides an opportunity for them to support each other as they speak to the group and each partner reports on one of the two states. For the poster presentations, another student in the class is called on to read the final statement about the two states. As the statements are similar across posters, the individual student who reads becomes familiar with the sentence structure even though the specifics are new.

Because two students working as partners produce the poster together, the individual student who speaks about a given state has had a great deal of prior scaffolding for this task. The joint efforts and social interaction between partners and, when necessary, with other, more knowledgeable classmates, provide essential and indispensable support (Vygotsky, 1978). The partners support each other in collecting, understanding, and preparing the information for the poster so that by the time individual students show the poster to the rest of the class and report the results, they are prepared to do so.

In combining the processes for learning through **oral transmission** and the **written word,** Christina consciously delivers her instruction by such techniques as reading aloud and pointing to the words as she reads. She applies this technique when describing the model poster as she indicates each specific section of the written version. She also reads each of the model sentences from the sentence frames aloud while students follow as she points to the words. For the students, there is constant oral interaction as they collect information in the computer lab from the bookmarked sites and as they compose the sentences together that will go on their poster. Finally, for the poster presentations, the students, following their teacher's model from the first day, explain their poster, indicating each section, and ask someone in the class to read the final statement of concession as they point to the words.

After considering which new **academic tasks** might be appropriate to link to her social studies lessons on the election, Christina has chosen to work with her class on the concept of comparison and contrast. Analyzing information in this way is new for them, but she knows they must master it for the many activities, assignments, and assessments they will encounter in school. In finding similarities and differences, she will have to be sure her students focus on specific details about the two states they are researching. For the final statement, which shows that a smaller state may have a larger number of votes, students will need to grasp a counterintuitive concept that develops their critical-thinking ability.

Christina also introduces the Internet as a tool for accessing data by searching for different information on carefully selected websites. Although her students have used the Internet and are familiar with computers, they may not have used websites for learning new material or for school-related activities. The central academic task is that of comparison/contrast, and the controlled Internet searching provides the necessary data.

By linking three academic tasks—gathering data, comparing/contrasting data, and interpreting data—Christina is building new formal schemata related to success in school. Critical thinking emerges from this because the result of this activity—that a larger state may have fewer votes—is generally counterintuitive to students. Thus, this activity, then, reinforces the importance of research and data collection to test intuitions and beliefs, an essential component of academic ways of thinking (Lee, 2005).

As Christina chooses to focus on the specific academic tasks, she needs to anchor them in **familiar language and content**. Scaffolding is needed for the SLIFE to direct their attention and effort to the new task. To start, Christina scaffolds the Internet searching. Using a webpage with her name on it, the students are directed to preselected sites with her brief annotations. Christina's use of a webpage tool allows the SLIFE to go to the selected URLs and search within one site for what they need. The sites she has located provide the information they need without a large number of mouse clicks, so they will not become frustrated with this new task. On the site, they see familiar language that Christina has prepared for them (see Chapter 7).

Visual aids are essential in teaching any ELLs but, once again, even more so with SLIFE. Christina has been teaching her SLIFE to read maps of their town and charts on familiar topics in preparation for more complex use of these visual supports. To scaffold the content about the election, Christina has many related visuals, including maps and population charts on the walls, for reference. She has prepared a diagram with the essential information of states and the number of votes they are allotted in choosing the president. The content for the lesson consists of state names, shapes, sizes, populations, and other data that are concrete and quantifiable, making the comparison and contrast accessible.

The language needed for collecting and reporting the data on the states is largely familiar to these SLIFE, as are the basic sentence structures SLIFE worked with earlier, such as X (*name of state*) has Y (*number of*) people. The only unfamiliar language structure is the statement of contrast with *although*, which is essential for grasping the counterintuitive concept involved in the contrast between densely populated small states and sparsely populated large ones. To make the new structure clear, Christina has ensured that each pairing of states results in this contrast. In this way, all the statements are similar and SLIFE can see them recurring, building familiarity with the structure. To scaffold the writing of their own statements, Christina refers the students back to the familiar individual statements of fact that underlie them.

As a result of Christina's careful preparation using the MALP instructional model, SLIFE can access the new and difficult academic tasks and concepts in her lesson. In this way, SLIFE are not limited in their exposure to such tasks, and they are not expected to perform them without being instructed in how to do so.

We see from this detailed analysis of MALP as it is integrated throughout Christina's lessons that this teacher has successfully internalized the model and put it to good use in ESL and Social Studies, producing a six-period, three-day sequence with social studies content and academic English language development for this group of students.

Using the MALP Checklist

How can teachers be sure they are using MALP in their lessons the way Christina did? To help, we have developed the MALP Checklist (see Figure 4.1 on page 68). The Checklist is an expedient and systematic way to be sure that the MALP instructional model is being used. It follows the three components of MALP. For each of these three components, there are two elements for the teacher to address while planning lessons and activities for SLIFE. The MALP Checklist consists of a series of statements for teachers to check off after they enter specifics from the lesson for each of the components of MALP. Teachers using the MALP instructional model look across the entire lesson sequence to see that all the elements of MALP are being implemented, rather than seeing each lesson as a separate freestanding period. Some elements will be more evident in one lesson, others in a different lesson, and still others across different lessons and days.

We turn now to another teacher, Rick, who is teaching MALP-based math lessons and is using the checklist to be sure all elements of MALP are included. As we follow Rick's lesson, we examine each of the six elements of MALP using the Checklist as a guide.

Math Scenario

Rick's self-contained math class for SLIFE is struggling with the language of math problems, as do many ELLs (Martinello, 2008). In addition, the SLIFE have very rudimentary math skills, yet they are still required to participate in a curriculum that demands that they move beyond basic skills. For example, Rick has been working on units of measurement, such as 12 inches being equal to one foot (12″ = 1′). The students have difficulty converting from one unit to another, such as changing 24 inches to 2 feet. Rick plans to use a concrete rather than abstract problem to demonstrate this and to give his students practice in working with units.

One day, Angel, who has been absent for over a week, returns to class, frustrated because he has found a part-time job in home construction but is having problems figuring out what his boss wants him to do. It turns out that the foreman expects Angel to help him measure floor areas and lay tile and carpet in a new office building.

Using Angel's experience as a starting point, Rick develops a sequence of lessons to help the SLIFE learn the math skills of measurement and converting units of measure. Rick's problem for the class is this: *How many tiles do we need to order for a house?* He begins by bringing in a diagram of his own house with each room labeled. For the purposes of this sequence of lessons, the class will use floor tile for all the rooms in the

FIGURE 4.1   The MALP Checklist (A. DeCapua & H.W. Marshall)

Mutually Adaptive Learning Paradigm – MALP Teacher Planning Checklist	
A. Accept Conditions for Learning	
A1. I am making this lesson/project immediately relevant to students.	☐
A2. I am helping students develop and maintain interconnectedness.	☐
B. Combine Processes for Learning	
B1. I am incorporating shared responsibility and individual accountability.	☐
B2. I am scaffolding the written word through oral interaction.	☐
C. Focus on New Activities for Learning	
C1. I am focusing on tasks requiring academic ways of thinking.	☐
C2. I am making these tasks accessible with familiar language and content.	☐

house. Rick has simplified the floor plan by ignoring closets, kitchen appliances, and other items that would create irregular patterns. In each room on the diagram, Rick writes the dimensions in feet and the tile size, large or small, that will be used for that room, as shown in Figure 4.2.

Rick also provides the class with a chart showing the dimensions of the two sizes of tile.

Tile Size	Tile Dimensions
Large tiles	12" x 12"
Small tiles	6" x 6"

FIGURE 4.2   House Diagram

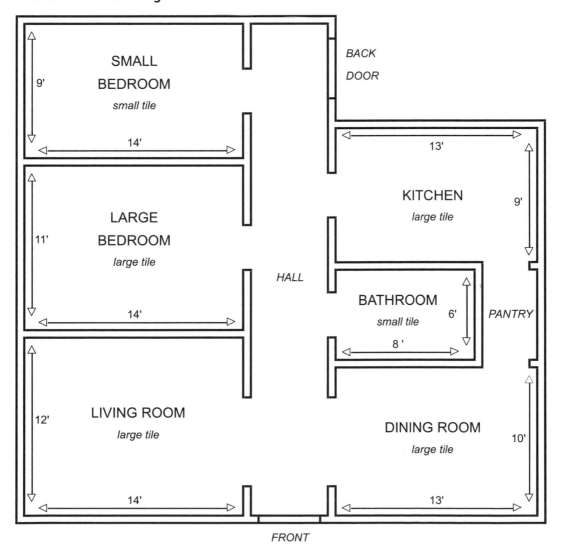

To help SLIFE visualize the problem, Rick brings in samples of tile and a photo of a room with a tile floor.

Finally, he posts a set of instructions with the sequence of steps they need to follow in order to find the number of tiles needed for one room of the house.

Steps to Solve the Problem

Follow these steps to solve the problem:

Step 1: Identify the question for the problem.

Step 2: Using the House Diagram, identify the dimensions of the room and the tile size needed for the room.

Step 3: Using the tile size and dimensions chart, identify the dimensions of the size needed for the room.

Step 4: Convert the dimensions to all inches or all feet.

Step 5: Determine the number of tiles needed for one row in the room.

Step 6: Determine the number of rows of tile needed for the room.

Step 7: Using mathematical operations, determine how many tiles are needed.

Step 8: Write the answer in a sentence and put a box around the number of tiles.

Rick has decided to break the problem into a series of activities designed to culminate in the class providing the number of tiles needed for the entire house. First, Rick and his students work as a class; the SLIFE select one room, the kitchen, to work on together. Rick points out the information given for the kitchen in the house diagram in Figure 4.2, that is, the dimensions of the room and the size of the tile. With Rick's guidance, the SLIFE use the steps listed and refer to the resources he has provided for them to determine the number of tiles needed for the kitchen floor. He provides sentence frames problems to guide them in this process:

Step 1: We must find out how many tiles we need for the _(name of room)_ floor.

Step 2: We see on the diagram of the house that the _(name of room)_ is _(dimensions of room)_ and _(small / large)_ tiles are required.

Step 3: We see from the tile size and dimensions table that the _(small / large)_ tiles are _(6" x 6"/ 12"by 12")_.

Step 4: We need to convert to the same unit. One _(small/large)_ tile is equal to _(foot number)_ by _(foot number)_.

Step 5: The room is _(length)_ long, so each row has _(number)_ tiles.

Step 6: Each tile is _(width)_ wide and the room is _(width)_ wide, so we need _(number)_ rows of tile.

Step 7: _(number)_ times _(number)_ = _(total number)_.

Step 8: We need a total of _(number)_ _(small / large)_ tiles for the _(name of room)_.

Rick's sample completed sentence frames are:

Step 1: We must find out how many tiles we need for the kitchen floor.

Step 2: We see on the diagram of the house that the kitchen is 9' by 13' and the large tiles are required.

Step 3: We see from the tile size and dimensions table that the large tiles are 12" by 12".

Step 4: We need to convert to the same unit. One large tile is equal to 1 ' by 1 '.

Step 5: The room is 13' long, so each row has 13 tiles.

Step 6: Each tile is 1' wide and the room is 9' wide, so we need 9 rows of tile.

Step 7: 9 times 13 = 117.

Step 8: We need a total of 117 large tiles for the kitchen.

At this point, we begin our analysis of Rick's lesson using the MALP Checklist as a guide. The two conditions for learning, immediate relevance and interconnectedness, are the two elements of Component A. The starting point for any teacher using MALP is to reflect on how these conditions will be established and maintained during a given MALP activity.

Discussion of Rick's Lessons

Rick: How am I making this lesson immediately relevant to my students?

In setting up his lessons, Rick has used a variety of techniques for the students to relate to the material. First, he takes his student Angel's experience in construction as his content for the math work. Angel shares information about his job with the class and describes the work he is learning to do for the construction company. For the problem, Rick shows them a diagram of his own family's house and a photo of a tiled floor in his house. He also brings in sample tiles. In this way, he links the lesson to real-world experiences.

Rick: How am I fostering interconnectedness and building a learning community?

Like Christina's lessons, Rick's classes also include many chances for students to interact informally and deepen their interconnectedness. During these lessons, Rick found that, in addition to Angel, several other SLIFE had had some experience with building materials. One student had worked as a carpenter's assistant; another was starting an after-school job in a floor-covering stock room. Because Rick allowed for free-flowing conversation, the students increasingly felt that this was a learning community where they, along with Rick, were creating something together. Rick brought in photos of himself in his home workshop, photos showing him with his brother in the act of laying tile for a room in his house, and a photo of the room before and after they laid the tile. These photos heightened the sense of interconnectedness between the SLIFE and their teacher. Depending on the teacher's background and experiences, the teachers can use other examples such as quilting, instead of using tiles like Rick did, that provide real-world examples of this math concept.

Rick makes time for activities that are not directly related to the curriculum because for SLIFE interconnectedness is a condition for learning. This investment helps SLIFE feel a sense of relevancy to an alien and unfamiliar classroom setting while building their basic literacy and language skills and learning some content. In addition, it serves to lessen the sense of cultural dissonance and encourages more positive involvement in the class overall.

To combine the processes for learning, Rick structures activities so that the processes from both learning paradigms are integral to his lessons. Rick finds ways to bring in oral language and shared experiences, all the while leading students to be individually responsible for part of the activity and to use their reading and writing skills to complete their work.

Rick: How am I incorporating both shared responsibility and individual accountability?

Rick's problem for the class requires the students to calculate the number of tiles for each room, add up the results, and then tell him how much tile must be ordered for the entire house. In order to accomplish this, the students will solve the problem in three stages, working first in teams, then in large groups, and finally as a whole class. Because construction tasks are by nature collaborative with various roles students can play, Rick organizes them into teams. Each team selects a room and signs up on the diagram Rick has posted to indicate which room they will calculate. Team 1 chooses to calculate how many small tiles they will need for the bathroom, and Team 2 for the small bedroom. Team 3 chooses to calculate how many large tiles will be needed for the living room, and Team 4 for the large bedroom.

Rick then breaks the problem into three parts:

1. Calculate how many tiles you need for your room.
2. Form a group with the other students who chose a room with small tiles. How many small tiles in total do we need for the house?

   Or

   Form a group with the other students who chose a room with large tiles. How many large tiles in total do we need for the house?
3. What is our final order of small and large tiles for the house?

When this class problem is completed, Rick assigns each student a similar but different problem to solve individually. This time, the students each measure a room in the school. For the new problem, each student decides whether to use small or large tiles. As support, the student can refer to the previous problem and to the steps.

Rick: How am I using oral transmission to scaffold the written word?

To introduce the topic, Rick begins with a short video clip that he found on the Internet. He plays it without the sound so that he himself can narrate it to control the language for his SLIFE class. The video demonstrates, step-by-step, the calculations needed for a building task. Rick pauses the video at selected points, writes key vocabulary and concepts on the board as he says them, and asks the students to repeat them. In this way, he highlights the academic language they will need, such as *determine, dimensions, convert*. Later, when the lessons continue with problem solving, the students will be prepared to discuss such problems because of this preteaching of the vocabulary.

Working together, the students discuss their own problem, using the words on the board that accompanied the video and Rick's voice. In addition, while one student goes through the math problem orally, step by step, another student writes it out for the group. Then another student reads it out loud to the group. When students present their results to the entire class, they explain the problem while pointing to the solution on the board, written out using the key vocabulary and concepts.

Rick: What new academic tasks am I introducing?

Rick intends to build ways of academic thinking into his math lessons, avoiding a focus on pure mathematical problem solving, although that, in and of itself, contains academic thinking. He looks to the academic tasks that underlie the math itself such as using charts and diagrams to locate relevant data and following steps in a sequence. Rick plans to strengthen the mathematical thinking of the SLIFE by first laying the foundation with these tasks. Because these tasks are new, however, he must introduce and practice them with language and content the SLIFE find accessible, gradually moving them toward the more challenging math concepts he must teach them, and the academic language that accompanies these concepts.

Rick thought that the construction project would be a great way to introduce and reinforce the concept of steps in problem solving for math and why order is important in getting to the final answer. Rick has decided to teach sequencing as the primary new academic task to focus on in this lesson. To scaffold this concept, Rick provides a clear list of the steps involved, which, especially for SLIFE, makes getting to the outcome of the problem easier and more efficient. To help the students visualize the problem, Rick uses the building materials themselves. He demonstrates how a construction task must follow a certain order.

Rick shows how other math problems they are solving also have a specific order to follow. He gives SLIFE a template similar to the one he used for the construction activity. SLIFE use this template as they work in teams to solve the problems. Because this sequence of problem-solving steps is new, the emphasis is to become familiar with this sequence, talk about it, write about it, and refer to it when they present their solutions to the class.

Template for Solving Math Problems

- Identify the given information.
- Determine what the question is asking.
- Identify the method you will use to solve the problem.
- Check to be sure the numbers you are using in this method can be combined (same units; like terms, etc.).
- Perform the operations one at a time in the correct order.
- Check that your answer makes sense.
- Draw a box around the final answer.

This template includes two items to which Rick must draw their attention: *Identify the method you will use to solve the problem* and *Check that your answer makes sense.* For the tile problems, the students did not need to be concerned with identifying the method to use for solving the problem because their teacher had provided the method. He points out that in future math work and on tests, they will be working on identifying the method to use for a given problem. Mastering this academic task is essential for their success.

Rick then explains to his class the importance of checking answers to be sure that they make sense. To illustrate, he uses the tile problem. The rooms are measured in feet but the tiles are measured in inches. In order to solve the problem, the students must convert all the numbers to the same unit, either inches or feet. To reinforce and practice, Rick shows them how ignoring the units will result in an error if the units are not the same. For example, in the kitchen, if they don't convert the tile from inches to feet and instead use the numbers 13 and 12 for their determination of the number of tiles needed in a row, they would get 156 tiles in one row and not 13 tiles. They can see in a concrete way that this is an unlikely answer. The importance of always checking an answer to see if it makes sense becomes a principle SLIFE now relate to and understand. They experience themselves what happens when all numbers are not converted to the same units.

Rick: How am I making the new tasks accessible to my students?

Rick has chosen a construction task to provide a context that is familiar. He uses the same language and content for all the problems the students work on rather than create new math problems, each of which provides a new situation with new content and vocabulary. While the linguistic complexity of math problems poses challenges for all ELLs (Martinello, 2008), this is even more true for SLIFE. Rick's use of the same language and content enables the SLIFE to focus on the academic task and not be distracted by unfamiliar language and content.

Rick shows a video but uses his own familiar voice and language to present it. Rick also writes key concepts on the board while pausing the video. Later in the lesson, Rick provides sentence frames to guide the students in producing their own language about the problem. Each of these techniques makes the academic tasks accessible to the SLIFE.

We have seen how Rick has worked his way through the MALP Checklist in his math lesson planning. Because he is incorporating the three components of MALP—the conditions, processes, and activities of the mutually adaptive approach—he is able to both support and appropriately challenge his class of SLIFE. The MALP Checklist helps teachers fine-tune their teaching, noting which elements are missing or need to be enhanced. Examine Christina's and Rick's completed MALP Checklists (see Figures 4.2 and 4.3 on pages 76–77).

FIGURE 4.2   Christina's Completed MALP Checklist

Mutually Adaptive Learning Paradigm – MALP Teacher Planning Checklist (Christina)

A. Accept Conditions for Learning

A1. I am making this lesson/project immediately relevant to my students.

- *Current event relevance: Election approaching – event in the news*
- *Geographic relevance: New York State – their state – is selected for the model poster*
- *Cultural relevance: A minority candidate is running for president – they are members of a minority group*
- *Academic relevance: Math class topic is estimating – population numbers can be estimated*

A2. I am helping students develop and maintain interconnectedness.

- *Teacher and students share personal connections to states selected*
- *Students talk about candidates and their opinions about the election*
- *Partners work together to gather information and make their poster*

B. Combine Processes for Learning

B1. I am incorporating both shared responsibility and individual accountability.

- *Pairs work together to collect required data*
- *Each member finds extra data for one state*
- *Pair produces poster with each contributing to the overall result*
- *Pairs present completed poster but each member discusses one state*

B2. I am scaffolding the written word through oral interaction.

- *Teacher's oral explanation of model poster while pointing to written version*
- *Teacher reading the model sentences aloud*
- *Students discussing the information they collected as they write it on the poster*
- *Students discuss the model sentences they are composing together*
- *Students explaining their poster while other students view written version*

C. Focus on New Activities for Learning

C1. I am focusing on tasks requiring academic ways of thinking.

- *Internet searching*
- *Comparing and contrasting*
- *Grasping a counterintuitive concept*

C2. I am making these tasks accessible with familiar language and content.

- *Guiding their Internet search by using delicious.com.*
- *Real-world content about the electoral college and the election scaffolded by maps, population figures and data collected*
- *Linguistic and critical thinking scaffolding by breaking down concession statement into individual statements of fact that underlie it*

FIGURE 4.3 Rick's Completed MALP Checklist

Mutually Adaptive Learning Paradigm – MALP
Teacher Planning Checklist (Rick)

A. Accept Conditions for Learning

A1. I am making this lesson/project immediately relevant to students.
- *Using a real-world problem from one of the students*
- *Linking math to specific skills students can apply where they live or work*

A2. I am helping students develop and maintain interconnectedness.
- *Students share experiences with building materials*
- *Teacher shares home workshop photos and experiences*

B. Combine Processes for Learning

B1. I am incorporating both shared responsibility and individual accountability.
- *Students work together on the first problem calculating the amount of tile.*
- *Each team is responsible for at least one room of the house for the second problem*
- *Teams combine into large groups to add up their results.*
- *Each student is individually accountable for at least one additional problem*

B2. I am scaffolding the written word through oral interaction.
- *Teacher narrates video while taking notes on board*
- *Students work out problems aloud while team members write*
- *Students read their work out loud while team members read along and check for accuracy*
- *Students present results orally to class with visual representation on board*

C. Focus on New Activities for Learning

C1. I am focusing on tasks requiring academic ways of thinking.
- *Students focus on the sequence of steps and the importance of a specific order*
- *Students consider how operations must have the same units to obtain the correct answer*
- *Students learn about checking their answers to see if they make sense*

C2. I am making these tasks accessible with familiar language and content.
- *Teacher provides video with his own narrative in familiar language and pauses video to write key concepts on board*
- *Teacher provides sentence frames to guide the use of language to describe steps of the problem*
- *Teacher uses familiar content of a construction activity for all the problems in the project*

─────────────── $\mathcal{F}$or Further Exploration ───────────────

Four teaching scenarios describing lessons designed for SLIFE are presented. Read at least two of these scenarios and then respond to the discussion questions.

Scenario A: ESL with Mrs. Boudreaux

Scenario B: Living Environment with Ms. Vargas

Scenario C: American History with Mr. Icoz

Scenario D: Estimating in Math Class with Mrs. Baldini

DISCUSSION QUESTIONS FOR THE SCENARIOS

1. What did you like about each lesson? Dislike?

2. What do you see as the strengths and weaknesses of each teacher?

3. Give specific examples of as many elements of MALP as you find in each scenario.

4. Identify elements of MALP that may be missing in the lesson.

5. Now, using the MALP Checklist in Figure 4.1, go back and analyze each scenario. You may find it easier to practice using the MALP Checklist by breaking up your analysis into three parts, based on the components of MALP:

   - Accept the learning conditions of SLIFE;

   - Combine the processes from both the SLIFE learning paradigm and the U.S. learning paradigm; and

   - Focus on new activities for learning—that is, new academic tasks, scaffolded with familiar language and content.

6. How did the Checklist help you in identifying which elements were present or missing? Explain.

7. Using the completed Checklist as a guide, provide suggestions for how the teacher could revise the lesson to include the missing elements that you have identified.

Scenario A: ESL with Mrs. Boudreaux

Mrs. Boudreaux's class is composed of 15 students, ranging in age from 15 to 20. As the bell rings, the students slowly come into class and find their seats. The room is pleasant, brightly lit from a bank of windows on one side. The desks are arranged in rows, with the teacher's desk in the front, off to the side. Because this is a SLIFE class, the teacher has modified the state English Language Arts curriculum.

After taking attendance, Mrs. Boudreaux begins her lesson by telling the students to get out the list of 15 vocabulary words that she passed out yesterday and that they were to practice for homework. The words were taken from a fairy tale the students had been reading. She pronounces a word and calls on a student to repeat it after her. Mrs. Boudreaux corrects the student's pronunciation and then moves on to the next word and another student. After doing this for a few words, the teacher asks the students, "Do you remember what this means?" indicating the next word on the list. When no one responds, she supplies the definition. For one word, *maroon*, Mrs. Boudreaux points to a student and says, "Ana, you know this word; what color is this?" Ana looks at her, puzzled. Mrs. Boudreaux turns to another student, Raul, and says, "Maybe you can help Ana." Raul points to Ana's sweatshirt and says, "maroon." Mrs. Boudreaux praises him and continues as she has with the remaining vocabulary words. After they have gone over all the words, Mrs. Boudreaux asks the students to choose any three words and to write one sentence using each word. To model this, she writes the word *market* on the board and asks, "Who can give me a sentence with this word?" Two students raise their hands; she picks one, Serge, and gives him the chalk. Serge writes, "I like to go to the market." She praises him and then reminds the class that they are supposed to do this on their own with their chosen vocabulary words from the list, repeating her earlier instructions.

Mrs. Boudreaux walks around the class as students work on this activity, checking their work. She stops at one student's desk, notices he is having problems completing his work, and repeats the instructions to him, "George, you need to pick three words [holding up three fingers] and write a sentence for each word. You need three sentences for three of these words," pointing to the list. Knowing that George is Haitian and assuming that he understands French, Mrs. Boudreaux then chooses one of the words, saying, "In French, this word is . . . and in French I can write this sentence with it," as she writes her French sentence. "Now you do this in English," she instructs George as she moves to the next student. The bell rings just after she has completed circling around to each student. She tells the class that their homework is to finish their sentences and that she will collect the homework tomorrow. Mrs. Boudreaux reminds them that it is important that they study these words because they will be on the test at the end of the week.

Scenario B: Living Environment with Ms. Vargas

In Ms. Vargas' science class for SLIFE, the students are learning to classify living versus nonliving things. Ms. Vargas reviews her earlier lesson on living versus nonliving things by projecting a picture of a jungle environment on the interactive whiteboard. She asks the SLIFE to point to some items they recognize and circles one of those items, a bamboo tree, and writes next to it "living" with a colored marker. Mrs. Vargas then has the students come to the whiteboard and circle other items that are examples of living things, using the same color marker. Next, she asks students to identify nonliving things on the slide. Ms. Vargas chooses one of these, circles it in a different color maker, and labels it "nonliving." She then has students come up again and circle these items, using the different colored marker.

Hanging on the wall are posters SLIFE created in a previous lesson on living and nonliving things. For living things, there is a list of defining characteristics for each. Ms. Vargas continually refers to this list during the lesson, reminding the SLIFE to think about each characteristic when they decide whether a given item is a living or nonliving thing. When one student becomes confused and identifies a rock as a living thing, another student points to the chart and reminds this student about the characteristics, for example, "No, rocks no breath."

After this review, Ms. Vargas projects a picture of a pond on the interactive whiteboard. She passes out copies of this picture and colored markers to the class. She then asks the students to identify to which group each of the different items in the picture belong, using one color for living and another color for nonliving. Together, the students consult with each other to label the items as living or nonliving things, again referring to the student posters, and working together to decide on which color to circle each item. When they have completed the task and showed their work to Ms. Vargas, she then instructs the students, "Each person choose one item and say whether it is a living or nonliving thing." Tell your partner at least one reason why it is a living or nonliving thing." When they have finished presenting their work to each other, Ms. Vargas announces that there will be a test the next day with a different picture depicting a mix of items. For the test, they will have to find, circle, and label each item as living or nonliving. They will also have to name the characteristics of living things without reference to the concept poster.

Scenario C: American History with Mr. Icoz

Just before the bell rings, Mr. Icoz hangs up a large poster of Abraham Lincoln on one wall and tapes two large sheets of blank chart paper to the blackboard. Mr. Icoz begins his social studies class by talking about the poster. He asks questions such as, "Who remembers who this is?" and "What did he do?" After a few minutes, Mr. Icoz points to the charts and tells the students that they are going to put information about Abraham Lincoln on the charts.

The first information on the chart, Mr. Icoz says, is going to be "What I Know" and the information on the second chart, "What I Want to Know." (We will refer to these as the K and the W charts, respectively.) He repeats the phrases as he writes them on the chart paper. He then asks the class what anyone remembers about yesterday's lesson on Abraham Lincoln. Margot shouts out, "I don't know nothing" to which Mr. Icoz responds, "I'm sure if you think, you'll know something about him. " Several of the other students are talking to each other in their native languages, Spanish and Creole, about some ideas. Soon Hennrick raises his hand and offers, "He was President of U.S. in 1860." Dadou jumps in and adds, "I see him on the money. He's on twenty dollar bill." At this point Blanca say, "He's on this money, también" and pulls out a penny from her pocket. Mr. Icoz then asks, "Does anyone have a twenty dollar bill? Or how about a five dollar one?" Sergio laughs and says, "We want the money but we got only the penny." Mr. Icoz takes out his wallet, finds two bills, a twenty dollar bill and a five dollar bill, and holds them up asking, "Okay, which bill has Abraham Lincoln on it?" Dadou says, "Oh, Oh, I wrong, he's on the five dollar." Mr. Icoz then asks Dadou and Blanca to each give him a sentence about Abraham Lincoln to put on the chart.

After they give him their sentences and he has written them in correct English, Mr. Icoz reads each sentence to the class and asks the students what else they can tell him about Abraham Lincoln. Graciela offers, "He is a white man but he help the black people freedom"; Jean, "He killed by bad man"; and David, "He against the slavery." Mr. Icoz continues this activity until the students have come up with ten sentences. He then turns the students' attention to the W chart and asks them what they would like to know about Abraham Lincoln. Victor says he wants to know, "Where he born"; Margot, "How did he became President"; and Hennrick, "How he free the black people." Mr. Icoz again writes all their sentences on the W chart and reads each one back to the class. He has the students break into groups of three and instructs them to come up with at least three additional sentences for the W chart. As the students work in their groups, Mr. Icoz circulates, checking to see that they are on track with the assignment. Once they have finished, he asks them to read their sentences aloud, writes them on the W chart, and reviews them again. When the bell rings, Mr. Icoz tells the class that tomorrow they will review these charts and begin working on a biography of Abraham Lincoln.

Scenario D: Estimating in Math Class with Mrs. Baldini

Mrs. Baldini begins today's lesson by passing out a worksheet. She points out the title, "Sums and Differences," to the students and says, "We're going to be connecting today's lesson with what we learned before about addition and subtraction. On this worksheet we see drawings of articles, such as a handbag and a T-shirt, with prices listed below each item." Mrs. Baldini calls on one student, Emmanuel, to read the first few items on the worksheet with the associated prices. She next calls on Lu to read more of the items, then another student, until the class has read through all the items and prices. When a student stumbles over the pronunciation of an item, Mrs. Baldini pronounces it and asks everyone to repeat it after her.

Mrs. Baldini draws the students' attention to the fact that the items and their prices are listed from left to right, rather than from top to bottom, as is more common in math problems. At several points Mrs. Baldini injects humor into the lesson by pointing out the oddities in some of the prices. A blouse, for instance, costs only $14.00, but a roll of tape is $5.00.

When the class has finished reading the items and prices out loud, Mrs. Baldini reminds the students of their previous lesson on estimating. She reviews the estimating process by picking the first two items and prices on the worksheet and estimating these numbers for the students. To make sure they remember the estimating process, Mrs. Baldini has the class work with her on estimating the next two prices. When she asks for a volunteer to lead the review on estimating with her, Emmanuel immediately raises his hand. The rest of the class watches quietly while Mrs. Baldini and Emmanuel round off the next two prices. When they have finished the review, she instructs the students to round off all the next five items on their own.

Once the students have completed these five, Mrs. Baldini reviews their work by calling on different students to provide their answers. For each response, she repeats the estimating process for that question. When Donni makes a mistake, Mrs. Baldini writes the numbers as she reviews the estimating process, step-by-step, prompting Donni to produce the correct answer. At the end of the class Mrs. Baldini assigns the remaining questions for homework.

5

Project-Based Learning

CHAPTER 4 EXPLORED HOW MALP CAN BE INFUSED into lessons by analyzing Christina's social studies lessons and Rick's math lessons in the context of MALP. Now is the time to introduce the concept that the lesson sequences of these two teachers were projects, the focus of Chapter 5. This chapter introduces and explores project-based learning, which is an effective way to implement the MALP instructional model. Project-based learning encourages immediate relevance and interconnectedness; allows for a great deal of differentiation; fosters group work while requiring individual accountability; easily integrates oral transmission and print; and provides a structure to introduce, practice, and recycle language, content, and academic ways of thinking.

Research on project-based learning indicates positive outcomes for diverse student populations (Carr & Jitendra, 2000; Ferretti, MacArthur, & Okolo, 2001). Project-based learning is ideal for SLIFE on many levels. Vygotsky (1962; 1978) argued that learning depends on social interactions and that instruction is best when it is learner-centered. Students are most likely to reach their optimal potential when they are engaged in relevant, socially interactive activities, with instruction scaffolded so that students are challenged yet able to reach the next level of knowledge. As they engage in project-based learning developed from their own needs and interests and are guided by their teachers, SLIFE develop the confidence to succeed and demonstrate to themselves, their peers, their teachers, and their families that they can indeed succeed in school (DeCapua & Marshall, 2010a, 2010b; Marshall & DeCapua, 2010; Marshall, DeCapua, & Antolini, 2010). Because project-based learning easily infuses the three components and six elements of MALP, the cultural dissonance experienced by SLIFE can be reduced. After the initial overview of project-based learning is presented in this chapter, Chapter 6 considers four short-term projects focused on specific types of academic thinking. Chapter 7 then explores in detail the implementation of one project designed to recur periodically throughout the year.

What Is Project-Based Learning?

Project-based learning centers on activities in which students produce something cooperatively over a period of time. A project may be as simple as producing a summary poster of key terms or may lead to a more complicated product, such as a monthly newsletter. The time period for any given project can range from one or two lessons to several months, depending on the type of project. Regardless of the duration, project-based learning serves to foster a learning community while promoting the acquisition of academic ways of thinking and content knowledge (Lin et al., 1995).

Although there are differences in approaches to project-based learning, the basic premises are the same. Project-based learning consists of learner-centered, active, and participatory activities; it is collaborative, integrates the four language skill areas (speaking, listening, reading, and writing), lends itself to an interdisciplinary approach, incorporates outside knowledge, results in a tangible product, and is long-term.

> *I don't know how to deal with such a mixed group [of SLIFE]. They range from preliterate to OK literacy but little content. How do I balance all their different academic needs in one class?*
>
> —Rob, ESL teacher, Atlanta, Georgia

A concern of many teachers of SLIFE is the range of abilities of their students and how to meet their needs. Project-based learning by nature allows for and accommodates differentiated instruction, as it consists of a series of tasks and activities that can be geared to a variety of student interests and abilities. For example, a project may encompass tasks ranging from oral (e.g., interviews) to written (e.g., summaries), to visual (e.g., photos) and on to publication (e.g., bulletin board display). Different students engage in those tasks that address their strengths and interests. In situations where students need to take on tasks that are beyond their capabilities, the nature of project-based learning promotes students supporting or mentoring one another, facilitated by the teacher.

Projects should be recursive. Although this is not an essential principle of project-based learning, we strongly believe that with SLIFE, projects benefit students the most when they are recursive. These projects avoid becoming repetitive and boring because, while the type of project remains the same, the topic of the project changes. For example, if students are engaged in iterative surveys, as described in Chapter 7, one survey may solicit information on people's favorite music artists while another solicits information on reasons for immigrating to the United States. Task repetition in the diverse contexts that projects provide fosters learning and control of language, retention of content knowledge, and the development and application of academic ways of thinking (DeKeyser, 2007), factors key to helping SLIFE achieve.

The principles of project-based learning are summarized:

Principles of Project-Based Learning
<ul><li>Instruction is learner-centered.</li><li>Teachers act as facilitators, advisors, and guides.</li><li>The classroom is dynamic and fluid, with group configurations changing in response to tasks, student abilities, and interests.</li><li>Project ideas develop from student interests and needs, but are based on required curriculum.</li><li>Projects are recursive.</li><li>Tasks allow for differentiated learning.</li></ul>

Oral Interaction in the Classroom

Meaningful interaction is central to the development of language skills and encourages students to become actively involved in the learning process (Gass & Mackey, 2006). Often, however, classrooms are dominated by teachers, minimizing the participation and engagement of students (Forestal, 1990). While this is of concern with all ELLs, it is especially true for SLIFE.

In addition, SLIFE frequently have difficulty paying attention when the teacher is interacting with one student because they do not necessarily grasp that U.S. teachers expect them to be active listeners—to listen and learn from the interaction even if they are not part of that interaction. SLIFE, in contrast, may simply wait for explicit questions or directions directed to them, and so much of the lesson will not be productive learning time for these students. Consider this example:

Mr. Harakla:	What's the first step to solve Number 4?
José:	See which number is bigger.
Teacher:	Yes, and María, tell us which one.
María:	[No response, after a few moments]: What's the question?

In the discussion of oral transmission in Chapter 2, we noted that SLIFE feel most comfortable when they are receiving messages with redundancy built into them. Although Mr. Harakla is trying to build on his exchange with José to include another student, María, he is unsuccessful. Such types of exchanges build on each other in a linear way so that if students miss the one-time input as in this example, they cannot participate. In this example, María does not see herself as part of a communicative chain and thus the exchange between teacher and student has to start all over again. María, and students like her, require a classroom community that minimizes the percent of time spent on teacher-student interactions. To engage María from the beginning, Mr. Harakla could have set the stage by modifying his initiation, using redundancy:

> *Mr. Harakla:*   María, we're doing number 4; the question is about the first step. José has said we need to find the larger number; my question to you is, Which number is larger?

This technique of building in redundancy to exchanges is a modification not commonly found in teacher-student exchanges (Cazden, 1988). The lack of such modifications is one reason why SLIFE instruction often becomes constant remediation and why so many SLIFE teachers feel that the students cannot, in effect, learn.

Teacher talk dominates the classroom but is not the type of talk that tends to promote successful learning among SLIFE. Teacher-centered classrooms discourage student-student interactions, which are not only important for developing language skills but essential in the MALP instructional model. Chapter 4 showed how Christina and Rick facilitated learning among their students through the implementation of MALP and project-based learning. Rather than traditional teacher-student question-and-answer patterns, Christina and Rick's lessons encouraged student interaction, either with each other or with them.

Project-based learning, as a learner-centered model, in contrast to teacher-centered teaching, encourages SLIFE to use real language for real needs. The students scaffold language and content for each other, using materials and tasks designed by the teacher to guide them. Because the teacher does not dominate in project-based learning, neither does teacher talk. Moreover, redundancy, clarification exchanges, and other elements of oral transmission are integral in project-based learning, providing a comfort level that is generally absent in classrooms dominated by such talk.

What Is a Project and What Is Not?

Although the concept of projects is not new, project-based learning is relatively so. Projects are central to the curriculum, and students develop their language and literacy skills and content knowledge within the context of projects. Projects are focused; teachers must clearly articulate the goals and objectives and make clear connections between the various activities and the skills and knowledge teachers expect their students to master (Barron et al., 1998). A project is different from a task or activity in that a project includes a sequence of planned tasks or activities. For example, if students are told to create a poster describing math sequences, that is a task. However, when this poster is the *culminating activity* of a series of lessons based on understanding the principles of math sequencing, then students have engaged in project-based learning.

For example, Mrs. Gomez has her students working in pairs to design a poster. The purpose is not only to solve a math problem but also to create a written version of the steps in solving this type of problem and the reasons for each step. The academic task objective is to provide support by giving reasons:

Steps	Reason
$10 - 2(3)$	We multiplied because the (3) is in parentheses and because it has a number outside the parentheses.
$10 - 6$	We are subtracting because we multiplied 2(3), and it gave us positive six. We put down 10 because it is negative.
(4)	We made a box for the answer. Solution = 4.

The time spent on the poster is time-on-task that engages the students and solidifies the concept they have been studying as they talk about their work together and practice writing. Mrs. Gomez has provided sentence frames to help them in their writing, and key vocabulary appears on a math word wall so that they can easily find the terms they need. The poster will have colors, designs, and other personalized additions, along with the content. Once the students have finished their posters, Mrs. Gomez puts them up on the wall so that students can refer to them as needed. When that math unit ends, she selects one or two posters to leave up. The sequence repeats for the next unit. By the end of the year, every student has at least one poster remaining up on the wall. The math concept posters are an example of a recursive short-term project.

Project-Based Learning and MALP

In project-based learning, the teacher acts as a facilitator and guide rather than as the repository of knowledge. Peer interaction and peer support, with teachers as guides, are central. In this approach, learning means *doing something*, not merely receiving and reproducing information. Chapter 4 examined Christina's three lessons that formed a project on the upcoming presidential election. On Day 1, the students shared their information about the states and ideas about the candidates. On Day 2, the students worked in pairs in the computer lab to find pertinent information; and on Day 3, the students worked on creating a poster. Because Christina functioned largely as a facilitator for the project and did not deliver teacher-fronted lessons with direct instruction, teacher talk was minimal, giving students heightened opportunities to engage in oral interaction.

Project-based learning does more than address the issue of teacher talk. Using project-based learning is consistent with MALP in that it meets the needs of SLIFE (Component A: Conditions), transitions them to the U.S. learning paradigm (Component B: Processes), and incorporates academic activities for learning (Component C).

Component A: Accept Conditions for Learning

The first element of Component A, immediate relevance, is fostered in project-based learning. Learning for all students is best accomplished when teachers engage their students in relevant, motivating, and challenging activities (Wells 1993). While there are many reasons why low-achieving students are not motivated to learn, a strong contributing factor is the feeling that school has little or no relevance in their lives (Schlossser, 1992). Because the projects are drawn from the interests and needs of students, they are of immediate benefit and relevance and, hence, are highly motivating (Bradford, 2005; DeCapua, Smathers, & Tang, 2009; Harris & Katz, 2001). However, while the goals of the project must be meaningful to students, students must also recognize the project as a realistic challenge that they can successfully carry out (Dörnyei, 2002).

Project-based learning is ideal for SLIFE because it allows for capitalizing on the pragmatic knowledge students have—their "funds of knowledge." In rural communities, children at a young age begin contributing to the family and gain extensive real-world knowledge that can provide the catalyst for classroom learning (Delgado-Gaitan & Trueba, 1991). Livestock and agricultural practices, food preparation, home medicinal care, and traditional crafts are excellent resources (Richardson et al., 2007). To take another example, Browning-Aiken (2005) describes how the family of one Mexican student, María, had passed on knowledge of the history of the Cananea mines, the working conditions, and issues of compensation, including details about a workers' strike there in 1906. In addition to this orally transmitted knowledge, María had more recent personal connections through her own extended family's experience with the subsequent closing of the mine where they worked. All of this pragmatic knowledge helped Maria become motivated to study geological processes and the history of the mining industry at school. Seeing the relevance to her own life and that of her family members, she could engage in studying about the environment and local history. The knowledge she brought prepared her to assimilate the new information she would receive in the curriculum unit at school.

In some cases, children who have not had formal schooling develop curriculum-specific skills that can directly transfer to what they will study in school. Saxe (1988) studied a group of Brazilian youth selling candy in the street who had developed math skills by negotiating prices with wholesalers and bargaining with potential customers. These pragmatic tasks coincide with specific mathematical operations and could prepare them for academic ways of thinking about those types of calculations in a school setting. Or, as we saw in Chapter 4, Rick's student, Angel, provided the catalyst for a math project with his need and interest in learning to measure and calculate floor space and tiles. With familiar cultural content linked to curriculum content, SLIFE sense **relevance,** the first element of Component A.

While engaging in projects, students help each other by providing assistance, encouragement, and shared interests, whether using their native language, English, or a combination of both (Foster & Ohta, 2005). Working together serves to develop interconnectedness and a sense of the classroom as a learning community, which meets the second condition of learning for SLIFE. Teachers as facilitators also serve to build this learning community. Low-achieving students are more likely to engage in the classroom and achieve academic success when teachers build relationships and connect to them on a personal level rather than acting as distant authority figures to their students (González & Ayala-Alcantar, 2008; Schlosser, 1992). It should be noted, however, that the sense of interconnectedness between teacher and students does not mean that teachers accept disrespectful and/or disruptive behavior. The teacher is still a person of authority and must be accorded respect.

During project work, the teacher is available and interacts with individual students and groups of students as needed. Although much of this interaction will center on content, there are opportunities for teachers to demonstrate a caring attitude, show interest in the students as people, and demonstrate respect for their knowledge, even when it is not the same as what is considered the norm by U.S. teachers. The resulting **interconnectedness** in a project-based MALP classroom provides SLIFE with the second element of Component A.

Mrs. Eckert's environmental science class is an example of a classroom learning community in which both SLIFE conditions for learning are in evidence. In this class, SLIFE learned about feeding relationships in ecosystems as part of their study of biotic communities and made diagrams illustrating the network of interactions and relationships of the flow of energy. They began by creating food chains, which are linear depictions of the flow of energy from one organism to the next, such as grass → cow → human. They then put these chains together into a food web. Because Mrs. Eckert had previously introduced the concept of comparison/contrast for this project, the students were able to describe a food web from their home country and compare it to the one they were learning about in their textbook. Some students came from the same region of the same country and were able to brainstorm together; others worked with students from different countries but similar ecosystems. In this example, we see how Mrs. Eckert accepted both conditions of Component A. By having the students share information about their own countries, they learned more about each other's backgrounds and strengthened **interconnectedness.** And, by having prior knowledge and new knowledge associated with the students' home countries, there was a sense of **relevance** to the standard science curriculum.

Component B: Combine Processes for Learning

In implementing Component B of MALP, teachers combine the familiar process of the learning paradigm of SLIFE, shared responsibility and oral transmission, with the new ones of U.S. schooling, individual accountability and print. As discussed in previous chapters, these processes come naturally to students who have been participating in Western-style schooling for a number of years and who come from cultures in which individual accountability and print are the norm. For SLIFE, project-based learning leads the way to their making the transition to individual accountability and print. Because project-based learning is based on interactive, participatory, and collaborative student engagement, much of the project work takes place in groups or pairs where students continually share ideas and plan tasks together. Nevertheless, SLIFE need to become individually responsible and accountable for their work; therefore, carefully planned projects include individual contributions. Christina's students **shared**

responsibility by working in pairs to gather information and plan their posters on electoral votes and state size. Yet, since SLIFE must learn to be **individually accountable** for their work, each of Christina's students prepared the material for his or her own state for the poster.

Too many students, too many levels. Don't know what to do.

—Derek, ESL teacher for science and math, New Jersey

Project-based learning requires many different tasks be completed for each project, which allows for a great deal of differentiation (see Chapters 6 and 7). Student participation is enabled by the ability of the teacher to differentiate assignments for the various language proficiency levels, literacy skills, background knowledge, and interests of learners. Because each project includes many different tasks, the pace of specific tasks related to the project, the explicitness or detail, and the nature of actual tasks can be adapted to student abilities. Teachers build in choices so that the SLIFE can select a task that seems accessible to them. As the year progresses, the teacher can guide that same student to more difficult tasks. In Christina's project on the election, students worked in pairs, helping each other to navigate the computer and/or websites.

Print is an essential part of any carefully planned project for SLIFE, supporting their transition from oral transmission to the written word. The transition from oral transmission to print occurs naturally during a project as there will nearly always be a written component designed for sharing their work with fellow students and others. Here, literacy is connected to something personally meaningful and significant to the students, motivating them to read and write (Guthrie & Wigfield, 2000). In Rick's construction project, oral interaction linked to literacy practice was evident. For instance, Rick wrote notes on the board as he narrated his video; later the students read their work aloud as others read along and checked for accuracy.

In another class, Mrs. Conti's ESL for SLIFE, the students were learning the English personal pronouns. In a traditional approach, students spend a great deal of their time completing practice worksheets. Mrs. Conti chose a different approach and elected to have the students practice the pronouns through a project. Each student would develop a simple PowerPoint presentation illustrating the English personal pronouns. For SLIFE, using PowerPoint is highly motivating since it encourages their creativity, while avoiding some of the difficulties these students face forming letters when writing by hand. However, such projects must be carefully scaffolded so that SLIFE can produce simple PowerPoint presentations.

To help her students, Mrs. Conti provided the students with a template for the presentation. This template consisted of a slide with a blank text box on the upper right, a blank text box in the middle, and another blank text box below. In the text box on the upper right, each student typed in one of the English personal pronouns. In the first text box in the middle, the student then typed in a sentence using this pronoun. (The students had previously worked on writing basic English sentences using different pronouns.) In the middle text box, the student placed a picture, photo, or drawing to illustrate each pronoun (see Figure 5.1 on page 92).

FIGURE 5.1   Deisi's PowerPoint Slide

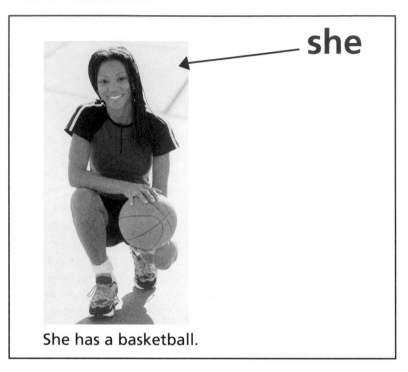

Deisi used the pronoun *she* and wrote *She has a basketball* below the photo she chose. Javier inserted a photo of his favorite brand of sneakers to illustrate his sentence, *They are shoes.* Maurice used a picture he had drawn based on a Manga character for his sentence, *It is a sword.*

In this PowerPoint project, **oral transmission** and **print** were consistently combined, one of the elements of Component B. In the process leading up to the creation of the projects, the students practiced writing and reading their sentences. As they presented their PowerPoint projects, they listened to each other and read what each one of them had written on the various slides. The second element of Component B is also evident, combining **shared responsibility** with **individual accountability**. In preparing their individual PowerPoint projects, the students shared responsibility. Students supported each other in learning the basics of PowerPoint and helped each other find representative pictures, photos, and drawings; yet, each PowerPoint established individual accountability because the final project was something each student had created that reflected personal choices.

Component C: Focus on New Activities for Learning

According to MALP, students must have frequent opportunities to develop and practice academic ways of thinking in the context of familiar language and content. A major benefit of project-based learning is the ability of the teacher to embed academic tasks throughout the project. Project-based learning allows for the development of higher-level thinking skills while expanding students' subject area knowledge. These higher-level thinking skills cannot be taught in isolation, but must be practiced and learned in the context of learning content. Willingham (2009) points out that if students are asked questions such as how they might feel about living in a rain forest, they will be able to provide thoughtful and analytic answers only if they have learned what the rain forest is, including information about climate, soil conditions, vegetation, and so on. If students don't have the requisite knowledge about rain forests, their responses are likely to be shallow—for example, "It would be rainy" (p. 37). Engaging in a project designed to build students' understanding of the ecosystem of the rain forest will provide them with the background for answering such questions and builds familiarity with the language and content. However, teachers need to be sure that projects are challenging, and not childish or "dumbed down." Although SLIFE, by definition, have limited or interrupted formal education, this does not mean that they do not have a great deal of other knowledge or that they are not smart (DeCapua, Smathers, & Tang, 2009; Gonzalez et al., 2005). A project can and must be challenging.

In summary, looking at project-based learning through the MALP lens, we see that it satisfies all the elements of the paradigm. It fosters interconnectedness by encouraging group work with individual accountability, combines the oral and print, and introduces and reinforces academic tasks by building on familiar language and content. It permits teachers to create meaningful learning, based on meaningful activities within the constraints of delivering the required curriculum, while developing the English language proficiency, content knowledge, and literacy skills of SLIFE.

Implementing Project-Based Learning

Like any effective instruction, project-based classroom work must be intentional—that is, the goals and objectives must be clear, and the instruction must be purposeful. Figure 5.2 illustrates various steps in a project. The steps before the implementation of the project ensure that the nature of the project, its instructional design, and its accessibility to the students will be in place. The steps following the implementation provide for the students and the teacher to see that the project has succeeded, or if there were difficulties, where they lie. This, in turn, informs future projects. Subsequent chapters discuss specific projects. For all of these projects, the cycle underlies the process and guides the teacher.

The first steps of the cycle consist of a planning process. This process begins when the students **brainstorm ideas for possible projects**. For SLIFE, the first few projects will need to be initiated by the teacher. Once the students become familiar with projects, they can suggest their own ideas or, alternatively, choose from topics the teacher provides. Once there is a list of possible directions to take the project, the students need to **select a focus**. If SLIFE are very limited in their English proficiency and there is no one working with the teacher who can help in the native language, the teacher may need to make this decision. In choosing a topic, teachers need to make sure that it is of high interest, relevant, and suitable for incorporating MALP. Once a topic

FIGURE 5.2   The Project Cycle

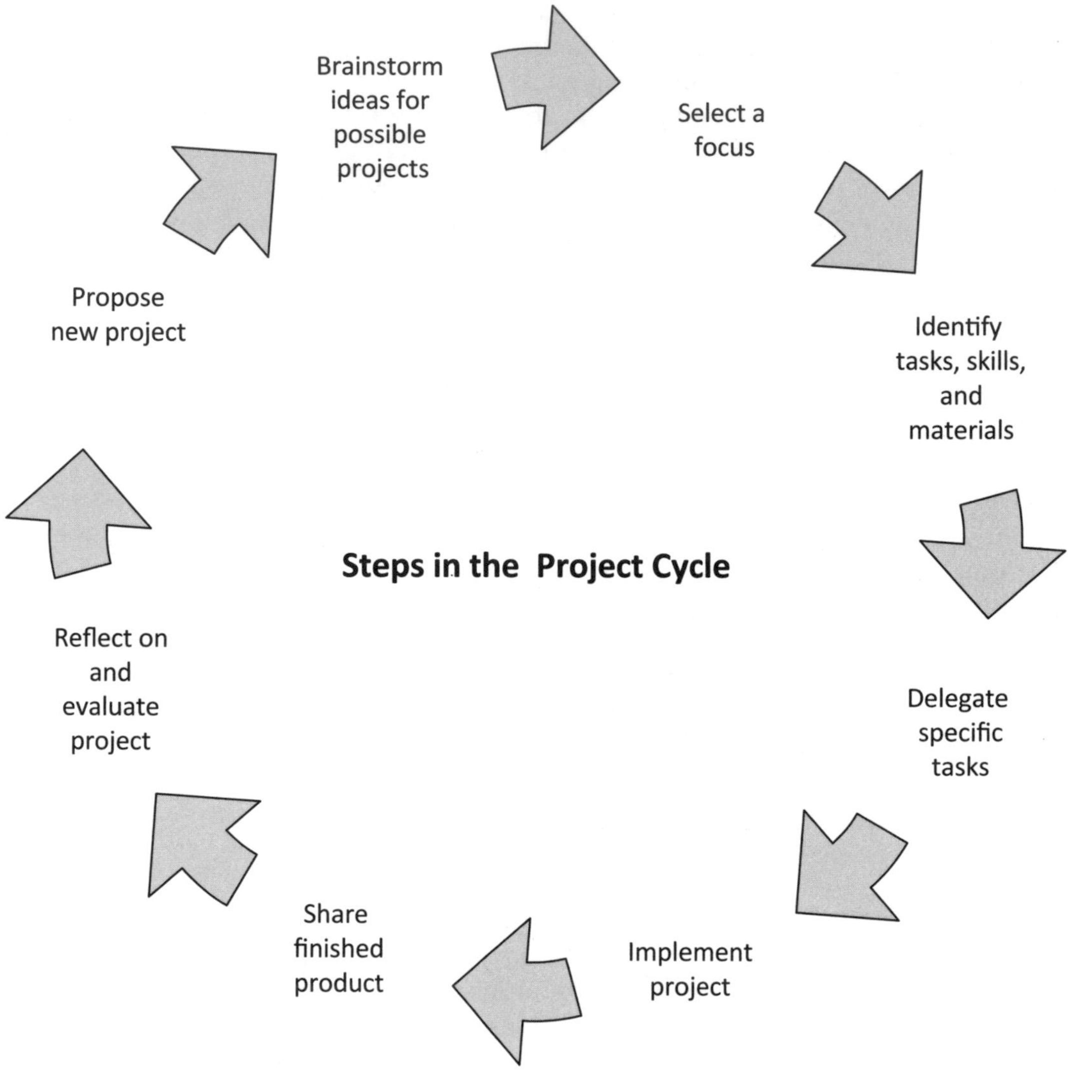

Brainstorm
ideas for
possible
projects

Select a
focus

Propose
new project

Identify
tasks, skills,
and
materials

Steps in the Project Cycle

Reflect on
and
evaluate
project

Delegate
specific
tasks

Share
finished
product

Implement
project

has been decided, the students and teachers **identify the specific tasks, skills, and materials** they need to execute the project. The next step is to **delegate specific tasks** to each student. For this step, students and teachers decide together who will be in charge of a given task based on the skills each student possesses at the time. Not all tasks need to be delegated at the beginning; as the project develops, students can choose to do (or be assigned by the teacher) different tasks, again depending on their interests and abilities. This is also the time to determine and obtain the necessary materials for use in the project.

Now the class is ready to **implement the project**. Here is the heart of the experience where SLIFE develop the new academic ways of thinking and practice the academic tasks underlying the specific project they are implementing. This can include, for example, sequencing, classifying, explaining, organizing, and evaluating information.

Once the project is completed, several follow-up steps help to establish the significance of the project. The first is for the students to **share the finished project**. This sharing can be with other members of the class, people in the school, or family and community members from outside the school. Or they may choose to post or publish a project or pieces to a class webpage.

Finally, the cycle ends as the students **reflect on and evaluate the project** both in terms of its design and its execution. For SLIFE with very limited proficiency, this can be as simple as asking them what they liked and didn't like about the project. For more proficient SLIFE, higher-order thinking questions can be asked, such as "What would you do differently next time about _____?" or "How might we make _____ clearer?" This final step in the project also becomes the first step for the next project, and the cycle repeats. Based on their reflections and discussion of the completed project, the class considers what other ideas may have arisen in the course of working on this project and/or in their reflections. Or, they may have ideas regarding another project that would help them grasp something in the curriculum. They are ready to **propose a new project**.

The scope of any given project will be influenced by the depth in which the teacher and/or students wish to explore a topic, the demands of the curriculum and of standardized testing, the length of class time, and many other factors. Nevertheless, effective implementation of MALP requires that teachers regard project-based learning as an organizing principle of effective SLIFE classrooms. Well-planned, project-based learning leads to in-depth, effective learning. It reduces the cognitive dissonance that SLIFE face. It helps teachers implement the three components of MALP.

Teachers can facilitate the successful implementation and completion of projects by continuously observing students to monitor their participation, check comprehension, and provide additional instruction, explanation, direction, information, and guidance as needed. Teachers need to know what, how much, how well the students are learning, and where there are difficulties and concerns that need to be addressed (Angelo & Cross, 1993). As SLIFE develop language proficiency and content knowledge and become comfortable with academic tasks and higher-level thinking, they become better able to manipulate information, and the projects can then become increasingly demanding and complex. To ensure MALP implementation across a project, teachers should make continual use of the MALP Checklist, Figure 4.1.

Project-Based Learning and the Curriculum

Faced with the realities of high-stakes testing, teachers may feel that project-based learning will detract from what they need to cover in the curriculum. In fact, just the opposite is true. Project-based learning encourages the integration and synthesis of interdisciplinary content knowledge (Colombo, 2002; DeCapua, Smathers, & Tang,

2009). If teachers regard the material in textbooks as departure points rather than as destinations, they will be able to work with students on projects that have relevance to and meaning for them (Clarke, 2007). For example, when students engage in class surveys (see Chapter 7), they can use the information they have gathered for developing graphs (Math), writing brief narratives (English Language Arts), researching more information on what they have found and/or using it as a springboard on related topics (Social Studies, Science), and so on.

Project-based learning also lends itself to developing content-area specific vocabulary. Mastery of content-area specific vocabulary is closely linked to academic success; yet such vocabulary presents a considerable impediment to SLIFE because of the number of terms needed to understand the various subject areas (Bielmiller, 2005; Moje, Collazo, Carillos, & Marx, 2001). Not only do SLIFE need to develop a large vocabulary, but even words with which they may be familiar have additional discipline-specific meanings. In math, for instance, *power* refers to the number of times that an amount is to be multiplied by itself. This is a very different meaning of *power* than what SLIFE would encounter in everyday use, where *power* is associated with control over people and things or strength or influence. A more related meaning is found in social studies where *power* is used to refer to the right or authority of government or institutions. Nevertheless, there are subtleties of difference that may not be easy for SLIFE to grasp initially. In project-based learning, vocabulary development and reinforcement is a natural product of the process. Vocabulary is not learned in isolation, and the recursive nature of projects allows for recycling of essential vocabulary, as well as concepts.

Well-planned and well-conceived projects motivate students to discuss, read, and write about concepts drawn from the curriculum, which can be woven into the projects, permitting for integration of knowledge rather than providing only isolated chunks of information. Another advantage of project-based learning is that it allows teachers to develop new knowledge as well as revisit and further develop material previously presented. As in Mrs. Gomez's math poster project, the students can refer to earlier posters when they get rusty on concepts already mastered and that are needed as the underpinnings for the current unit. Rather than have a teacher say, "We did that last month, you should remember. Check your notebook," the scaffolding from past to present has been provided by their fellow students and is on display in the classroom.

Some teachers may associate projects with organizational chaos and a lack of concrete learning outcomes. In project-based learning, teachers function as motivators, facilitators, and instructors. As motivators, they construct joint projects with the students, helping students identify topics of interest. As facilitators, they ensure that students know what they are supposed to do and when, and they provide essential content and language knowledge (Van den Branden & Verhelst, 2007). As instructors, they carefully develop learning outcomes based on the curriculum, the needs and abilities of the students, and the topic of the project. Thus, project-based learning, when carefully structured by the teacher, allows students to use language in authentic situations and provides rich opportunities for learning both language and content (see, e.g., Van den Branden & Verhelst, 2007).

Furthermore, the MALP instructional model suggests that projects be recursive. Once a solid foundation to project-based learning has been constructed, less class time needs to be devoted to the "how" of a project. As students become accustomed to project-based learning, the basic organizational processes will have become familiar, and more time can be spent on the execution of the project. Likewise, as SLIFE become more familiar with basic academic tasks, such as compare and contrast and categorization, projects will move along faster.

───────────────── 𝒇or Further Exploration ─────────────────

1. If you are a teacher, record or videotape one of your classes. Alternatively, observe a class that is not your own. If you are not a teacher, find a class to observe. How much teacher talk versus student-student talk took place? What suggestions can you offer to increase the amount of student talk? Give at least two specific techniques.

2. Think back to your own learning experiences. Were you ever involved in project-based learning? What was your reaction to project-based learning?

3. Interview at least three teachers and ask them if they are familiar with project-based learning. If they say yes, ask them what they know about project-based learning. Ask whether they currently implement, or have implemented, this approach, and their reasons for doing so or not.

4. Look at previous lessons you have taught or you have observed someone else teach. What projects might you incorporate? Come up with at least two ideas.

5. If you have implemented a project in a class you have taught, try to complete the MALP Checklist (Figure 4.1) for this task. What modifications would you need to make it a successful project for SLIFE?

6

Projects Targeting Academic Thinking

THIS CHAPTER LOOKS AT PROJECTS with a focus on Component C, which asks teachers and students to work together on academic ways of thinking. This component is critical because teachers must address academic ways of thinking in order to transition SLIFE to U.S. schooling since these ways of thinking are essential if students are to succeed academically. As previously emphasized, Component C requires teachers to focus the attention of SLIFE on new activities for learning. These activities consist of academic tasks and must entail academic ways of thinking, rather than the pragmatic ways of thinking more common to their prior learning experiences.

First let us review what is meant by academic tasks and academic ways of thinking, concepts generally associated with Bloom's Taxonomy mentioned briefly in Chapters 2 and 3. In its original conception, the taxonomy identified six levels of complexity of thinking (Bloom, 1956) from least complex to most complex: knowledge, comprehension, application, analysis, synthesis, and evaluation. Bloom's Taxonomy was later revised to align with more recent research about learning. While the six levels of complexity remain, they were slightly reordered and renamed (Anderson et al., 2001). The names of the levels were also changed from nouns to verbs to reflect their active use in learning objectives. In the revised version, the six levels are: *remembering, understanding, applying, analyzing, evaluating,* and *creating.* Both the original and revised versions of Bloom's Taxonomy succinctly outline levels of cognitive engagement, accounting in part for its popularity.

For SLIFE, all of the levels of complexity entail ways of thinking that are unfamiliar as understood in the context of formal education. For example, defining is considered part of the act of remembering, and yet, for SLIFE, defining a tree is neither a common learning task nor a meaningful one. Summarizing is considered part of one's ability to demonstrate understanding but is another new task for SLIFE. Similarly, for each of the levels of the taxonomy, the tasks required are new and challenging for SLIFE. Therefore, teachers need to focus on tasks at all of the levels and scaffold them carefully for these students.

To make these new tasks accessible to the students, teachers embed them in language and content that is familiar to the students from previous work or from their own real-world experience. To review, the third component of MALP, with its two elements, appears on the MALP Checklist (see Figure 4.1 on page 68).

Why Target Academic Thinking?

While all of the projects discussed here are implementations of the entire model, they are designed with specific academic tasks in mind. Secondary teachers generally assume that by the time students are in high school, they are familiar with scientific practices and academic ways of thinking (Lee, 2005). High school SLIFE, however, have not had the benefit of learning and practicing such thinking, so it is essential that teachers of SLIFE introduce and practice these academic ways of thinking so that students become accustomed to and comfortable with them. The projects provide teachers with practice in the third component of MALP—focus on new activities with familiar language and content. Teachers can select a particular project related to the type of academic thinking on which they intend to focus with the SLIFE at that time.

These projects should be implemented using the Project Cycle (Figure 5.2). Readers should keep these steps in mind as they proceed through the four projects discussed. In addition, given that the focus here is on academic tasks rather than on the other components and elements of MALP, readers should extract these other components and elements from the narratives of each of the four projects. Doing so will provide meaningful practice in recognizing the components of MALP and identifying the elements of each.

For the purposes of MALP activities, we have selected some ways of academic thinking that are unfamiliar to SLIFE. We have used these to develop the four short-term MALP projects presented in this chapter. The academic tasks targeted in these projects are

Classify

Compare and contrast

Define

Evaluate

Explain

Sequence

Summarize

In addition to these, teachers can refer to detailed lists of the academic tasks associated with each of Bloom's levels of cognitive engagement (e.g., Krathwohl, 2002; Marzano & Kendall, 2008) to create similar projects, depending on which types of academic thinking they wish to develop. These projects can be implemented with any level of language and literacy proficiency if they are appropriately scaffolded and supported.

What is important to keep in mind with respect to MALP projects is that in addition to focusing on the traditional areas of language and content, the goal of teachers of SLIFE should be to build new schemata for these unfamiliar ways of thinking. The four projects in this chapter are designed to focus specifically on one or more of these ways of thinking, while not neglecting language and content. Table 6.1 on page 100 lists these four projects, the academic tasks they target, and sample project activities.

TABLE 6.1
Projects, Academic Tasks, and Sample Activities

Project	Academic Tasks	Sample Activity
1. Mapping Time	Sequence	Timelines
2. Collections	Classify Compare and contrast Define	Mystery Bag
3. Autobiography	Evaluate Explain	Transitions
4. Bookmarking	Classify Evaluate Summarize	Delicious.com

By now, readers have a clear grasp of the MALP instructional model and how it should be infused into lessons for SLIFE. Project-based learning is the optimal way to implement all six elements of MALP. However, since all teachers are not able to devote the requisite time to elaborate learning experiences as class surveys, we present four projects that require minimal time to implement and carry out. Properly implemented, these projects can turn any classroom with SLIFE into a MALP classroom.

Mapping Time

For this project, the academic task is sequencing, and the sample activity described is Timelines.

Mapping Time	Sequence	Timelines

SLIFE come to our schools with very different experiences and understandings of the world. SLIFE often tend to live in the here and now, and are less concerned with the past and future. Many of them come from agricultural backgrounds and follow different rhythms, ones that are less based on the clock and less on the daily, weekly, monthly, and yearly compartmentalizing of time than is the norm in mainstream U.S. society (Martinez, 2009). The compartmentalization of time that U.S. teachers take for granted is not something SLIFE are necessarily familiar with or accept (Jegede, 1994). Furthermore, because their access to formal education has been limited, SLIFE are frequently unaware of historical events, whether in their own country or in the world at large. Thus, one of the roles of teachers of SLIFE is to develop a sense of linear, historical time. Mapping time is an indispensable concept for SLIFE and focuses their attention on the academic task of **sequencing**.

Timelines

The most common activity associated with mapping time is creating a timeline, namely a linear representation of the occurrence of events over a specified period of time. Timelines can easily be incorporated into many lessons, and they are a very simple, yet effective way of introducing and fostering the sense of time expected in U.S. schools. A timeline can be a simple graphic representation of student dates of arrival in the U.S. or a very elaborate description of important historical events around the world. Timelines can be created early in the school year and added to as new events occur in the lives of the SLIFE or as they learn new information. Timelines should be posted where the students can see them and where they can use them as resources.

We suggest that teachers of SLIFE begin with timelines that show personal information and other events that the students deem important. Personal timelines provide immediate relevance and encourage interconnectedness, as students share their information with each other while developing an academic and U.S. way of conceptualizing time. Once SLIFE have mastered the concept of timelines, they can be used for many different topics in the curriculum. Teachers can use them in science to illustrate the geologic periods, or in English Language Arts to show the chronology of the life and works of an author.

A personal event that features prominently in U.S. culture is one's birthday, yet the importance placed on birthdays is not universal. In some cultures, one's name day is celebrated rather than one's date of birth; in others, only the year is important (year of the rabbit, for example). And for others, neither may hold significance. Thus, teachers may encounter SLIFE who are unaware of their birthday and/or who may have been assigned an approximate one upon arriving in the United States.

Mrs. Aquino decided that by creating a timeline activity focusing on birthdays, she would include cultural information that would enhance the experience of her newly arrived SLIFE. First she conducted lessons on the months of the year and on the cardinal and ordinal numbers from 1 to 31. Mrs. Aquino gives each student a small poster with a template on it that has two sentence frames and asks them to work in pairs to complete their posters. In the U.S., the month is stated before the day: *January first*. In many other countries, the day is noted before the month: *first January*. Given that some of Mrs. Aquino's SLIFE are used to the latter, she is careful to bring this difference to their attention before they work on these sentence frames. The following lesson excerpt occurs after her students have mastered these lessons.

> My birthday is on the _____ day of _____.
>
> My birthday is _____ _____.

In using sentence frames with ELLs, teachers often present more than one frame as a way of providing choice. In this case, however, the two sentence frames actually represent two steps in the process of producing the sentence as native speakers would say it. The first frame is the scaffolding; the second is the final form. In this way, the teacher is breaking the new formal schema of how the date is stated in English into pieces. Working in pairs and using the word wall where the months are listed for reference, the students decide on what to enter in the blanks on the poster. The first sentence frame provides the scaffolding for the second one.

Once the students have completed the posters, their next step is to decide with a partner whose birthday comes first. After each pair has finished and verified with Mrs. Aquino that they have done this step correctly, she asks the students to arrange themselves physically into a class timeline. In other words, the students line themselves up in the front of the classroom in order of their birthdays. Collaboratively, the students examine the posters each pair is holding up for everyone to see and arrange themselves in the correct chronological order. In so doing, Marcel and Yamaris discover that both their birthdays fall in November. To determine their place in the timeline, they have to take the extra step of ascertaining whose birthday comes first in November. With the help of the other students, Marcel and Yamaris decide that Marcel, whose birthday is November 12th, comes before Yamaris, whose birthday is November 21st. This step reinforces cardinal number recognition and practice, and time sequence.

After the students have finished the physical timeline, they continue to stand. One by one and in order, they say the date of their birthday to Mrs. Aquino as she creates a written timeline by entering these dates from left to right on a blank timeline she has drawn on the board. When the students have all had their turn, Mrs. Aquino tells the students her birthday and asks them to indicate where it should be placed on the timeline. For further practice, the students practice saying the dates and the months, while looking at the timeline on the board. Mrs. Aquino sums up the activity by explaining that they have created a timeline, a visual representation of time order.

We see how this project has focused on a key academic way of thinking: **sequencing**. Later in the month, Mrs. Aquino builds on this initial timeline activity and has the SLIFE create another timeline with the birthdates of various historical persons about whom they are learning.

Calendars

Calendars are also often new for SLIFE, at least in the ways that we use them to mark dates and events, and as reminders to ourselves. Mrs. Aquino, to help her SLIFE become more familiar with calendars and time reference, especially in relation to mapping, puts a large month-by-month calendar up on the wall, and the students enter their respective birthdays on the appropriate day and month.

1. **Explain how producing a timeline and then a calendar as Mrs. Aquino does with her SLIFE is scaffolding.**

2. **What are some other items for which you could use the calendar with your class of SLIFE?**

Fostering both the ability to conceptualize time as linear and the awareness of the importance of time, dates, and schedules in U.S. culture can help SLIFE in subject areas such as social studies and history, as well as reinforce the importance of school schedules.

Collections

For this project, the academic tasks are classifying, comparing and contrasting, and defining. The sample activity described is Mystery Bag.

Collections	Classify Compare and contrast Define	Mystery Bag

To participate successfully in U.S. schooling, SLIFE must learn to perceive categories and groupings, as well as similarities and differences within those groupings. Recall the examples from Chapter 2.

In addition to perceiving categories, defining terms and concepts is a basic component of most classes across the whole curriculum and in every grade level. One of the most common questions asked in U.S. schools is, "What is X?" (Heath, 1983; Pridham, 2001). For low-proficiency ELLs including SLIFE, the response to such a question is often either a translation of that word into their native language or an example of the word, rather than a definition. In the case of SLIFE, it has been our experience that there are two major contributors to such responses. First, SLIFE, like other ELLs, lack strong English language skills. Second, and more significantly, SLIFE have not fully developed academic ways of thinking. For these students, such a question makes little sense because defining something based on abstract categories or concepts is an unfamiliar academic task. To address this issue, the mystery bag activity introduces SLIFE to the act of defining by teaching them about classifications and salient characteristics.

An excellent starting point to introduce academic thinking is to create a class collection of items. These items should share some essential characteristic for classification purposes but differ in ways that are not important for classification purposes. Many items lend themselves to collections in different interests and content areas, and do not need to be expensive or elaborate. Teachers can use collections of rocks, seashells, fossils, books, hats, magnets, bottle caps and jar lids, or coins, to name just a few. For example, Ms. Schaefer has a collection of turtle objects—turtles out of stone, wood, seashells, and straw, of all different colors and sizes, and manufactured in many different countries. Some of these turtles are purely decorative while others are paperweights, staplers, candles, soap, magnets, or have some other practical use. Despite the many differences, these figures are all still recognizably turtles. She will use this collection to develop familiarity with ways of academic thinking.

The Mystery Bag

The Mystery Bag is based on collections and introduces and/or reinforces three academic skills: **classification, compare and contrast,** and **defining**. In this activity, the teacher introduces the concept of a collection by giving each student a bag with one object inside. Only she knows that each student has an item representing the same type of object, such as Ms. Schaefer's collection of turtles. The students are instructed to examine their object without removing it from the bag so that no one else can see it. The teacher then guides the students through a series of questions about their object. For yes/no questions, the students respond by raising their hands. For the open-ended questions, the students respond orally. After each question, the teacher writes the results on the board. Gradually, as the students see these results, they begin to realize that they all have the same object, even though there are many differences. In Ms. Schaefer's class, although the objects in each student's Mystery Bag differ in size, shape, function, material, and so on, they are still all turtles.

Sample Mystery Bag Questions

- What is it?
- Have you ever seen one before?
- Where have you seen it?
- Do you know what it is called in your native language?
- What are some words to describe it?
- How does it move?
- How does it sound?
- What do you use it for?

Working through these types of questions helps SLIFE develop an understanding that, despite differences, there is one salient characteristic common to everyone's object. This, they come to see, forms the basis of scientifically based **classification**. Once SLIFE have developed a sense of classification, Mrs. Schaefer focuses on comparison and contrast. She has the students remove their objects from their bags and leads them in a discussion of similarities and differences. The students discuss how the turtles are similar and different from each other: overall appearance, origin, material, function, and so on, listing adjectives and other descriptive words on the board as they come up.

After students have examined the similarities and differences of their objects as a whole class, Mrs. Schaefer introduces a more targeted **comparison and contrast** task that further reinforces using academic language and ways of thinking. Working in pairs, the students prepare to talk about the two turtles they have and how they are the same as or different from each other.

A final step in this project is to practice the concept of **defining**. To develop their academic language proficiency and academic ways of thinking, SLIFE need to practice providing more than one-word definitions. To scaffold the task, the teacher provides sentence frames that are commonly used for simple definitions. As a class and with the teacher's help, students produce a few definitions. In defining turtles, Ms. Schaefer's class came up with these definitions.

A <u>turtle</u> is a <u>reptile</u> that has <u>a hard shell</u>.

A <u>turtle</u> is a <u>reptile</u> with <u>a hard shell, four legs, and a tail</u>.

A <u>turtle</u> is a <u>reptile</u> that <u>swims</u>.

Students used these sentence frames:

A/an _____ *(the object)* is a/an _____ *(the category)* that has _____.

A _____ *(the object)* is a/an _____ *(the category)*, with _____.

A _____ *(the object)* is a/an _____ *(the category)* that *(verb)*_____.

This type of guided sentence practice gives SLIFE the theoretical underpinnings of defining so that they move beyond copying or memorizing a sentence from a dictionary or glossary. The teacher can close the activity by having SLIFE practice defining other vocabulary words, either ones chosen by the teacher or suggested by the students.

While the collections project is especially suited to science classes, it can be used with other content areas as well. What is most important is that students develop classification, compare/contrast, and defining skills—skills that they need in all content area classes.

Autobiography

For this project, the academic tasks are evaluating and explaining, and the sample activity described is Transitions.

Autobiography	Evaluate Explain	Transitions

Autobiographies are a popular activity for ELLs because autobiographies are meaningful to students and draw on what they already know (Pierce & Brisk, 2002). As a MALP project, the autobiography becomes more than a way of depicting a series of life events. The teacher structures the autobiography in such a way as to bring into focus some aspect of one's life that, in turn, can be subject to critical thinking. A list of

ways to provide structure to an autobiographical project is to include a focus on influ-
ential people in one's life, special places in one's memory, or, as is the case with the
sample project presented here, life-altering experiences or transitions.

Transitions

In this project, SLIFE find specific times in their lives when important events occurred,
and they made choices. Students research their own lives, something immediately
relevant to them. At the same time, when they share their projects, they learn about
what is most important to each other, causing them to become more interconnected.
The display for this project can be a flow chart, a bar graph, an oral presentation with
visuals, or a written description. The key is to display the insights gained from the
process of reflecting on transitions. The project requires academic ways of thinking,
as the students need to reflect on which events and choices were the most important to them, and then analyze those events and choices in terms of why each was
significant.

The project begins by identification of events in their lives. This activity asks that
they **evaluate** which events were truly transitions—events that changed their lives in
some important way. To introduce the concept of transitions, Mr. Park compares an
event that was a transition to the action of opening of a door and going through the
doorway to a new place. Using the metaphor of a doorway helps his students relate
the concept to their lives. Several of Mr. Park's students, for example, mention their
coming to the U.S. as a transition in their lives. Others mention the birth of a sibling.

Once the SLIFE have the general idea of a transition, Mr. Park turns their attention to the focus of his transitions project, At My Door. The students focus on one turning point in their lives when they made a difficult decision. First, they give examples
of difficult decisions people have to make in their lives such as getting married or
starting a new job. Next, they talk about people they know who have made difficult
decisions. Mr. Park tells them about his decision to become a high school ESL teacher
after 10 years of working for the phone company. Then, they work together to talk
about their own lives and several difficult transitions that they have had to make.
After they have had some time to share significant decisions with each other, each
student selects one decision to examine in more detail. Mr. Park asks his class of SLIFE
to elaborate, requiring students to develop and practice the concept of **explaining** by
providing support, which is essential to academic work. Because this is an autobiography project, the focus is on the individual, and students will need to generate their
own explanations, but the students can work as partners or in groups to assist each
other in elaborating on their transitions.

The students learn that to explain in an academic way, they need to ask themselves specific types of questions. The answers to those questions will provide an
explanation of their decision. To guide them, Mr. Park provides his students with a
template for their description and analysis of the chosen transition. He has developed
five questions to help the students explain and evaluate their transition. Using the
questions on page 107, the SLIFE are able to analyze what happened as they stood at
their doorway and then, to reflect on the aftermath of going through the doorway.

Sample Transition Questions
1. What was the transition?
2. What were the choices?
3. Who helped you make this transition?
4. What happened as a result of this transition?
5. How would your life be different if you did not experience this transition?

Miranda is one of the students who chose coming to the U.S. as her transition. On the template provided by Mr. Park, she filled in keywords to indicate her responses to the five questions, as shown.

Transitions Project—At My Door	
Questions	**Key Words**
What was the transition?	*come to U.S.*
What were the choices?	*stay in my country* *come to U.S.*
Who helped you make this transition?	*my father*
What happened as a result of this transition?	*live in U.S.* *go to school* *learn English*
How would your life be different if you did not experience this transition?	*live in my country* *see my grandmother* *not know English*

In this project, SLIFE have the opportunity to develop the academic tasks of **evaluating** and **explaining.** Miranda is developing these academic ways of thinking using familiar language and content. Once she has answered these questions, she can apply this type of thinking to other topics that are less familiar. The academic ways of thinking introduced and practiced with this project will be useful for teachers in other subjects where students need to learn about the relative impact of specific events or ideas. For example, in math class, this can be used to practice making graphs. Students can make a list of the major transitions in their lives and then rate them on a scale of 1 to 5 as to how important they were in their lives. Next to each, they write the date, or if they are not sure, the approximate time or their age when each of these events occurred. Using the ranking for the y-axis and the dates or ages for the x-axis, the SLIFE enter points on the graph and label each point by drawing a picture or writing a word to describe the transition. In this way, the mathematical concept of graphing points becomes familiar and relevant, and each student is able to share important events with fellow students.

Looking at the transitions in their own lives serves as a basis for SLIFE to engage in thinking across the curriculum by helping them become comfortable with commonly asked questions that demand such thinking. When their teachers ask "why...?" or "what if...?" or "how...?" SLIFE will now be familiar with the type of responses expected and will be more likely to contribute to class discussions.

Bookmarking

For this project, the academic tasks are classifying, evaluating, and summarizing, and the sample activity described uses delicious.com.

Bookmarking	Classify Evaluate Summarize	Delicious.com

The last project targeting academic ways of thinking is a technology project, which takes place entirely on the computer. This allows SLIFE to become familiar with using the Internet, as well as with using academic ways of thinking to perform new tasks on the computer.

Embracing Technology

Integrating computer technology in project-based learning is essential given that familiarity with computers is so common in today's world. Teachers sometimes feel that because school is so challenging for SLIFE, it would be a mistake to add technology into the mix; however, the reverse is actually the case. We have observed many SLIFE classes in which the students see the possibilities of using technological tools for their projects and embrace them. Computer skills enhance student engagement and increase their ability to perform such tasks as writing (Cummins et al., 2007; Mendrinos, 1997). Computer skills can be as straightforward as creating the basic PowerPoint presentations mentioned in Chapter 5 or as complex as creating an interactive webpage. The use of technology becomes part of the project, so the students naturally share expertise and find ways to problem solve for each other. Students can ask each other and the teacher, and/or a lab technician if the learning is taking place in a staffed computer lab. Again, the interactions build community as well as computer skills and the language and content included in the project become embedded as students prepare written versions of their work.

As another example of incorporating technology into the classroom, consider the interactive whiteboard. Such a tool allows users to move objects around and to hide and show them at different times. In Mr. Johnson's school, the science curriculum called for students to learn about cells. Before SLIFE could do so, they needed to learn how to use a microscope. As a project, one group in Mr. Johnson's content-based ESL class for

SLIFE produced an interactive "book" for the whiteboard with different "pages." One page depicted the different parts of the microscope, another demonstrated how to use a microscope, and other pages presented photos of what one can see under a microscope. The interactive nature of the whiteboard allowed SLIFE to show their mastery of the topic by creating activities on the microscope for their fellow students.

In addition to the hesitancy about technology based on the perceived limitations of SLIFE with regard to computers, there is the belief that time spent on technology takes away from the development of language and content. Again, however, time spent in which SLIFE are interacting, discussing ways of presenting material, and building confidence increases the likelihood of their staying in school and ultimately succeeding there (DeCapua & Marshall, 2010a, 2010b, 2011; Marshall & DeCapua, 2010). Furthermore, although initially time spent on technology may decrease the formal time allotment for developing language and content, the skills that SLIFE learn thereby are invaluable in today's world. These skills serve to ease some of their difficulties, such as forming letters and basic handwriting skills.

Delicious.com

The impetus for this project was a lesson we observed in which students were placed before computers and told, "Type in the web address from the index card in front of you and hit Enter." As the SLIFE were new to literacy and as the web address was very long, they had difficulty getting it typed correctly into the address bar and getting to the site. In addition, once at the website, they struggled to take in what they saw on the page, as the many links and options overwhelmed them. We watched and listened, noting their frustration but also noting their strong desire to conquer this new technology and be able to access the sites and information that they needed.

This project examines a shortcut that provides students with an effective way to manage their Internet searching and offers ideas of how to build toward more complex and personally tailored computer use. Delicious.com, owned and operated by Yahoo! since 2005, is a web service for social bookmarking that provides a web space to store and share web addresses, called bookmarks, making them accessible from any location. While we use delicious.com as our shortcut here, readers will understand that because web technology changes rapidly, they will want to adapt and update the specifics accordingly, given that anything written about using the Internet in classrooms can quickly become obsolete. Nevertheless, the spirit, if not the letter, of the project designed for this class may be taken and used as a MALP project when adapted to new technological tools.

For this project, teachers set up a webpage on delicious.com for their class on which they include links to some sites related to what the class is studying. This is called a "bookmarking page." The address of the bookmarking page is very short and easy to enter: http://delicious.com/name.

Initially, teachers should put links to only two or three carefully selected sites on the page. The page will include the teacher's name and the links, each with an appropriate title. Teachers can write short summaries of the content of each site in the Notes boxes below the titles and then decide on some important keywords, called "tags," to help students organize the sites. In this way, the students are connected to the content and learn about bookmarking, titles, and keywords.

Figure 6.1 shows Ms. Anton's bookmarking page created especially for her social studies class of SLIFE. Because her SLIFE were learning about Abraham Lincoln, she selected sites about him. To save each new bookmark, Ms. Anton entered the site's URL to make a link, gave the link a title, wrote a short note or summary of the site, and selected tags that would group the site with similar ones. Using the Edit button, Ms. Anton can continue to add more tags, such as Civil War or biography.

When students click on a tag, they see all the links that have that same tag. If, for example, Ms. Anton's class also studied George Washington, her bookmarking page might have the tag "presidents" for links to the sites about Washington. They can also search on delicious.com using the tag to find links to other sites that users of delicious.com have tagged with "presidents."

Tagging is a useful feature of bookmarking that SLIFE can learn how to do relatively easily. It helps students understand the concept of keywords introduced across the curriculum and is a valuable skill that directly leads to categorization and showing relationships among ideas. A given link will become part of a group of links that relate to a meaningful category for the student. Multiple tags show how ideas are interrelated and can be categorized differently depending on one's focus. This is a very concrete way to practice this type of academic thinking, using familiar topics and concepts but thinking about them in a new way.

As teachers have their students continue their work on the selected topic, the students can add their own links about the topic, and add notes and tags for each. Thus, this becomes a **classification** task and enables teachers to help SLIFE become more adept at placing individual items, in this case links, in a valid classification.

FIGURE 6.1   Ms. Anton's Bookmarking Page

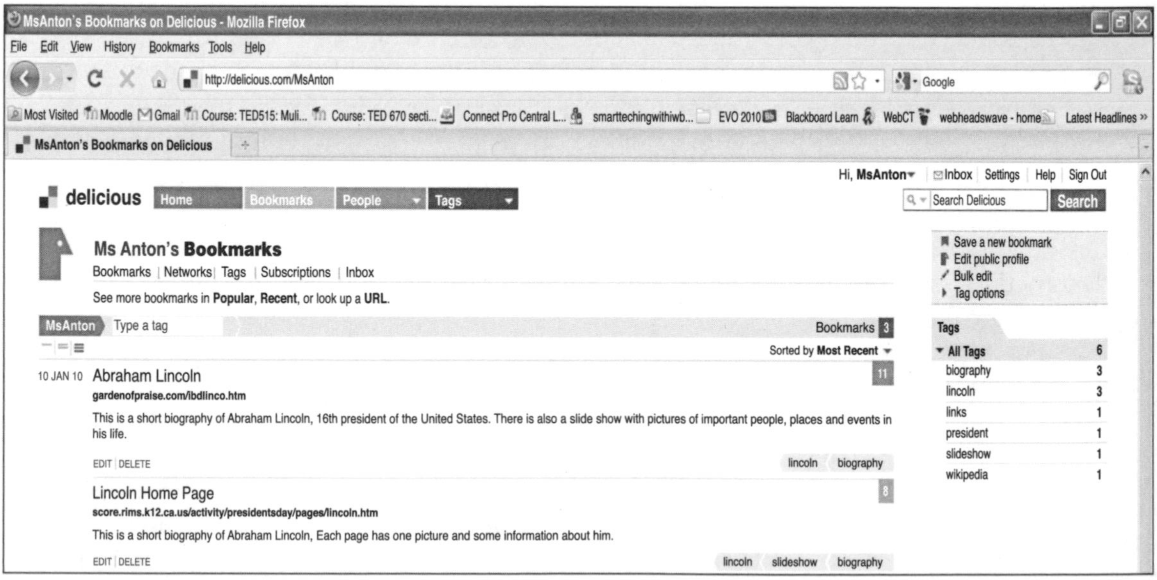

Once SLIFE understand the concept of bookmarking and have become comfortable using the computer and the Internet at this basic level, teachers can help the students create their own bookmarking pages. To ensure success and minimum frustration on the part of SLIFE who still have difficulties with literacy, both computer and print, this must be carefully scaffolded. The first step is the concept of having one's own page. Some students may already have a page on Facebook or some other Internet application and can explain that idea to their fellow students. Like other individual webpages, the student bookmarking page will have a web address, but its content will only be shared at the discretion of its creator. Each item on the page can be made available to other specific audiences, or to no one, as indicated in the settings set by the user.

Once each SLIFE has created a personal bookmarking page, the next step is to add bookmarks. After Ms. Anton's SLIFE had finished learning about Abraham Lincoln, she had them research famous people from their own countries. To help them do so, she added headings for each country and links to descriptions of famous people from that country. Later, as the students were creating their personal bookmarking pages, they decided that they wanted to include links to sites for their countries onto their pages, so they copied the appropriate links from Ms. Anton's page. To organize their bookmarked sites, they added tags, using their teacher's bookmarking page as a model.

A further next step in a bookmarking project is to have students personalize their bookmarking pages by finding their own sites on a topic of interest to them. This becomes an **evaluation** task, as they learn how to determine which sites provide the best, or the most accessible, information for the topic.

Ms. Anton's SLIFE were, like most teenagers, very interested in music, so Ms. Anton had each student find a link to a site about a favorite artist and add the link to his or her personal bookmarking page. Once the SLIFE had selected the links they chose to bookmark, they needed to decide on their own tags or use the ones suggested by delicious.com. One student, Ana, for example, included links to her favorite music sites on her page, and she added tags, such as *salsa, Dominican*.

In addition, for each site selected, Ana wrote a brief **summary** of the site and why it would be interesting or useful to visit. Ms. Anton scaffolded the summaries for the SLIFE by walking them through the summaries on her own bookmarking page. Writing a summary of the material on a webpage about a familiar topic helps SLIFE become skilled at this important academic task.

The bookmarking project can be expanded to include learning how to visit each other's pages and sharing links. Sharing links has potential for projects requiring research if students are working in groups and each student has a particular topic. They can assist each other if they find a source for another student and, rather than email the link, they can simply place it on their bookmarking page and share the link. To share a link, the students add each other to their networks on delicious.com so that they can see each other's links.

Once SLIFE have mastered the bookmarking tool, they can use it as a resource for research in any of the content areas. In Mrs. Salazar's class, the students were engaged in a survey project on music. Visiting each other's pages, sharing links, and tagging "favorite music" prepared them to visit each other's music sites, compare and contrast them, and eventually evaluate them, based on the questions from the survey they were conducting.

These four sample projects all focus on specific academic tasks while also incorporating the other elements of MALP. After completing one of these projects, teachers may decide to include an additional step, a debriefing of the activity. Integrating a debriefing phase can be very important as it encourages SLIFE to become aware of the specific new ways of academic thinking they have practiced in the activity. Such questions as, "Why did we do this activity?" or "What new skills did you learn that you can use?" may assist them in making the connections to their other schoolwork. If such transfer of learning possibilities are not made explicit, SLIFE may not take advantage of them. They could, for example, simply recall that, "We stood in line." "We looked at some turtles in a bag," "We talked about something that happened to us." "We used the computer." *Talking about* thinking is, we believe, as important as the activity itself so that students become accustomed to thoughtfully and purposely analyzing their thought processes.

These four are examples of short-term projects that teachers can adapt and adjust to their own students and their own curriculum. They can also become iterative if teachers want to implement them in different contexts, or if different subject area teachers decide to implement them on their own. SLIFE benefit from redundancy as they work toward mastering the academic ways of thinking that are manifested by the academic tasks included in these projects. Moreover, as the year progresses, the same projects can be made more complicated and the tasks embedded with more difficult material, further moving SLIFE toward academic success.

The activities on page 113 ask you to reexamine these four projects to see how they might be altered or expanded for additional practice. The flexibility of MALP allows for many variations on these projects. The key is to follow the MALP Checklist to ensure that all elements are included and that the mutually adaptive intent of the three components of this instructional model is carefully followed.

$\mathcal{F}$or Further Exploration

1. Suggest other objects that could form collections for the Mystery Bag activity. Think of examples relevant to different content areas, such as math, social studies, and English Language Arts.

2. Hughes & Greenhough (2006) describe an assignment where students took home an empty shoebox to decorate and fill with objects of personal importance to them. The teacher also filled her own box to provide students with glimpses into her life outside of school and to foster interconnectedness. The contents of these shoeboxes were used in different subject areas. For math, for instance, the students weighed and measured different objects from their boxes while for English Language Arts the students wrote about the different items.

   a. How do you see this project as fitting into the MALP instructional model? Be specific. For example, what academic tasks do you think you could incorporate into such a project?

   b. The objects in the box were used in different classes for different lessons. Can you think of how these objects could be used in your subject area?

   c. Explain how this shoebox activity could be developed into (1) a time mapping project; (2) a collections project; and (3) an autobiography.

3. The delicious.com activity focused on one technological tool, bookmarking, and how it can develop the academic thinking of SLIFE. Describe another technological tool you know that might also be the subject of a MALP project and that would help SLIFE with skills they can transfer across the curriculum. Explain how this tool exemplifies MALP by using the six elements of MALP. Show how you would incorporate these elements, and, in particular, what academic tasks you would incorporate and scaffold with familiar language and content.

4. Chapter 4 discussed the importance of having academic task objectives, in addition to language and content objectives. Go back to each of the four projects in this chapter, and create at least one academic task objective for each project.

5. Refer to the MALP Checklist as a guide, and review each project.

   a. Looking at Components A and B of the Checklist, think about how the timeline project allows for accepting the learning conditions of SLIFE and combining the processes from both learning paradigms, the paradigm of SLIFE and that of the United States.

   b. If you don't see a given MALP element addressed explicitly, think of at least one example of how that element could be incorporated into the project.

7

Sample Project—Class Surveys

THIS CHAPTER PRESENTS ANOTHER TYPE OF MALP PROJECT, class surveys; in this case, the project can become a regular part of the class and routine throughout the year. By *survey*, we mean any question or set of questions posed to a group of individuals to provide information that can later be presented, summarized, analyzed, and discussed. Surveys are a common and very successful ESL teaching technique, one that is especially appropriate for SLIFE (see, e.g., Cohen, 2009; Nunan, 2003). This chapter examines surveys in detail to show how SLIFE have created, conducted, analyzed, and reported on surveys and how their work exemplifies the implementation of MALP.

Why Class Surveys?

Surveys are uniquely suited to the backgrounds and needs of SLIFE. In fact, we believe that surveys constitute the single most valuable activity for SLIFE as they transition to formal education and literacy in English. The steps involved in the survey project incorporate the conditions, processes, and activities necessary for a mutually adaptive approach to the instruction of SLIFE. Both conditions for learning, immediate relevance and interconnectedness, fit well with the survey project. Students select topics that interest them, and they find out more about each other's interests and opinions by asking the questions of each other. Students provide support and encouragement for each other as they undertake the survey. The processes for learning, oral transmission and print, combine naturally as each step of the survey project provides for both oral and written components. Similarly, shared and individual responsibility can be delegated for specific tasks so that the teacher can vary these processes for a particular class and a given survey.

Surveys, as any type of project, allow for differentiated instruction because students can take on different tasks depending on their interests and abilities. An additional benefit is that almost any material can be incorporated into surveys and adapted to any proficiency and literacy level of SLIFE. The acts of creating, conducting, analyzing, and reporting on a survey allow for implementation of MALP. The information gathered in surveys can be used as the basis for any number of lessons in different content areas. Surveys can be conducted many times during the year, building in redundancy so that students become accustomed to this type of project.

In addition to being an excellent way to bring SLIFE toward Western-style education, surveys are an important part of U.S. culture. Opinion polls and reports appear everywhere, with opportunities to analyze trends and data. Large collections of opinion polls and surveys on a variety of subjects, for example, can be found at the Inter-University Consortium for Political and Social Research (ICPSR) and at Cornell University's Institute for Social and Economic Research websites. Much of the factual information in the media today is supported by survey data that can be understood by those who have some ability to decode it. Full participation as citizens is enhanced by this ability, and beyond their academic benefit, surveys provide a springboard to more participation in the world at large (Oskamp & Schultz, 2004).

Survey projects can be repeated weekly, monthly, or at intervals that coincide with the curriculum. Surveys can be related to events occurring in the school or in the community that generate interest, or even to issues in the wider world that students raise in class. The built-in redundancy ensures that all SLIFE will become familiar with the academic tasks of the survey. The iterative nature of this project is what makes it so powerful for building increasingly higher levels of comfort with academic ways of thinking. The continuous launching of survey projects throughout the year also gives everyone a chance to learn and participate, regardless of attendance issues, language proficiency level, or other factors that might impede progress without the opportunity to revisit the tasks again and again. The level of difficulty of each task can be determined by the topic, by the students' English language proficiency, and by their literacy skills.

Finally, and perhaps most important, the survey helps develop skills in carrying out academic tasks, scaffolded by familiar language and content. To create a survey, students generate and sequence relevant questions, presenting them in a variety of formats, quantifying the responses, finding patterns, and reporting the results in an organized form. At the same time, the topic and questions come from material previously studied or nonacademic material related to their lives, so that the schemata are balanced but with an emphasis on the formal schemata of the academic tasks.

The 7 Steps in a Survey Project

- *Step 1:* Select the topic.
- *Step 2:* Create and organize the questions.
- *Step 3:* Conduct the survey.
- *Step 4:* Analyze and quantify the data.
- *Step 5:* Draw conclusions.
- *Step 6:* Report on the survey.
- *Step 7:* Disseminate the results.

Undertaking class surveys entails following a series of seven steps and coordinating the tasks in each step in a seamless manner. Each of these seven steps contributes to the overall goals of building the ability of SLIFE to conceptualize academically, use language academically, and perform new academic tasks. The steps move the students smoothly through the process so that they experience firsthand an introduction to academic ways of thinking. Guided by the teacher, the students learn how to develop from start to finish what is essentially a mini-research project.

The long-term goal is for each individual student to perform all seven steps. The teacher begins by modeling and guiding the students as a whole class, step-by-step through the process. The class uses *The 7 Essential Steps in a Survey Project*, which is posted in the classroom as a resource to help remind students of the steps and for them to check where they are in the survey process.

Any of the seven steps of survey projects can be completed by the teacher, the entire class, groups of students, partners, or individual students. These various configurations allow for differentiation based on the abilities and interests of SLIFE. In addition, because MALP survey projects are iterative over the course of the year, students have the opportunity to implement a variety of tasks relating to each step, as they feel confident and ready to perform a given role in the survey projects.

As the students become familiar with the steps of a survey project, a group of students, partners, or even a single student can be responsible for an entire project. The various steps in the process of creating questions, collecting the data, analyzing the data, and presenting the data can also be easily and flexibly delegated to either groups or individuals, depending on the specific configuration of the class. The important point to keep in mind is that at least some of the tasks, some of the time, require each individual in the class to be separately accountable, facilitating the transition from shared responsibility to individual accountability.

Teachers may wonder how long a survey should be. There is no set number as to how many questions to include on a survey. A beginning survey can have as few as two or three questions; later in the year, there may be much longer surveys. In working with SLIFE on developing survey questions, teachers need to judge a reasonable number by the students' rate of progress, the time available, the language abilities of the students, and other factors. The actual number should be kept flexible so that SLIFE can take ownership of the survey length as well as the topic and questions.

Introducing the Concept of Surveys

An excellent way to introduce the concept of surveys is to start with an informal one in which the teacher asks the students a few questions, has them respond by raising their hands, and tallies their answers on the board (Cohen, 2009). Mrs. Restauro introduced surveys to her ESL class of high school SLIFE by asking them what they like to do in their free time. They each contributed ideas, which she listed on the board.

Then Mrs. Restauro conducted a brief survey. For example, she asked, "Who likes to talk on their cell phone?" After the students responded, she wrote the tally on the board and asked another question, "Who likes to listen to music?" noting again the tally on the board, as shown.

Who likes to...?		
Activity	**# of People**	**Total**
talk on a cell phone	𝍷𝍷𝍷𝍷𝍷𝍷𝍷𝍷𝍷𝍷 //	12
listen to music	///	3
watch TV	//	2
play video games	𝍷𝍷𝍷𝍷𝍷	5
# of students in our class: 12		

After Mrs. Restauro finished with the questions, she showed the SLIFE how individual responses are aggregated and totaled to find patterns. Next, Mrs. Restauro asked students why they might want to have this information from a survey. At first, they were not able to tell her, but then someone in the class said, "What kind of music?" And another said "rock" and so on, which led them to start talking about music groups and styles. She then pointed out that surveys can help them to get to know each other, share ideas, and learn from each other. This was a good start. Once the students have formed an idea of what surveys are, the class is ready to begin its first one.

We now move through the seven steps in this MALP project, noting the incorporation of the MALP elements: immediate relevance, interconnectedness, a combination of both shared responsibility and individual accountability, and both oral transmission and the written word, and a focus on academic tasks with scaffolding through familiar language and content.

Step 1: Select the Topic

The first step is to select a topic for the survey by brainstorming ideas with the students. To align with MALP, topics should have **immediate relevance** to the students. The survey topic can directly relate to a unit that the class has completed, zeroing in on an area the students would like to know more about. Alternatively, the survey can address topics of interest to the students that have no connection to school, such as personal tastes in food or music. Because the project is designed to accomplish a partial paradigm shift in learning and its most essential element is to concretize the formal schemata of academic tasks, the content, although important to the teacher and students, is not the central focus of surveys at this point.

With curriculum-based surveys, students decide on content-related topics and questions that interest them, which exemplifies content-based ESL instruction in the MALP model. The survey can give SLIFE the opportunity to make the connections between the curriculum and their own lives and satisfy their curiosity about the curriculum. Surveys draw from the KWL technique, which was originally introduced by Ogle (1986) to guide students in reading a text but which has since expanded to many different classroom learning situations. On a KWL chart, each letter represents one of three areas of focus: **K** = what I already know; **W** = what I want to learn; and **L** = what I have learned. Under KWL, teachers first work to activate students' prior knowledge by exploring with them what they already know about the given topic. Then students, working together as a whole class or in small groups, decide what it is they want to learn, which ensures relevance. After the students have investigated the topic they want to learn more about, they summarize what it is they have learned. Surveys focus on the W portion of the chart.

Perhaps the most critical criterion in selecting a topic is to make sure that it is a familiar one to the students. For students to focus specifically on the new **academic tasks**, teachers should conduct the surveys based on the content at the end of a unit so that any content and language needed for background to the survey is already familiar to them. MALP surveys are intended to provide students with the opportunity to continue processing curriculum that they have already been exposed to in class.

For example, at the close of an American history unit on immigration, Mrs. McKeogh's class of SLIFE developed a survey on that topic. The students had been learning about the many ethnic groups present in the United States and some of the issues arising from the diversity. Mrs. McKeogh had introduced two contrasting perspectives on this diversity, the notion of the U.S. as a melting pot versus the U.S. as a stew (or a salad bowl), and the students decided to include a question on this in their survey. The topic was related directly to the curriculum and yet was also immediately relevant to the students. *Which is best: melting pot or stew?*

Another question the students generated was related to immigration and the school and the community: What is the biggest problem for new immigrants?

Surveys can also address material unrelated to the curriculum, yet of immediate relevance. For example, the survey could treat a topic related to the school itself. A teacher can use the survey for the SLIFE to become more familiar with the school and the teachers. In this case the topic is close to the students' current experience so they will be able to generate relevant questions. In Mr. Pinella's social studies class for SLIFE, students wanted to understand better what teachers and the administrative staff thought about problems new immigrant students faced in their school and came up with the this: *What is the Number 1 problem for new immigrant students in this school?*

Surveys do not have to be opinion polls. A survey may entail collecting data on facts about the school or its students, such as how many years each teacher has been teaching. Mr. Pinella's SLIFE wanted to know which teachers in their school, if any, spoke their language or, perhaps, had studied it at one time: *What languages do you speak?*

To summarize, whether the survey content comes from previously studied curriculum or nonacademic topics the students choose to investigate, the main guideline is for the content to be familiar. In this way, SLIFE will focus on the academic tasks involved in the activity itself.

Although the class can develop a survey project about any topic, there are some guidelines to follow since the goal is to have SLIFE succeed academically. One factor in deciding on a suitable topic is that survey content must be appropriate to the age and status of SLIFE as high school students. As with many school-sponsored activities, teacher judgment and school policy will determine what constraints might apply. Teachers will want to steer students away from topics that may be of interest but would involve more resources and more time than is feasible, so as not to discourage SLIFE who are new to data collection. For example, if the SLIFE wanted to survey opinions regarding court cases and immigration laws, teachers might suggest they limit their survey to an opinion poll of one issue of particular concern, such as the deportation of illegal immigrants. Nevertheless, there remains a wide range of possible directions the class can go in designing surveys that promote language and literacy skills, develop academic ways of thinking, and mitigate the sense of cultural dissonance SLIFE experience.

Step 2: Create and Organize the Questions

Once the topic is selected, the next task is to create the survey questions. Regardless of the survey topic, the students, working with the teacher, develop a set of questions on a topic they would like to find out more about. The entire class can generate questions together, groups can generate questions, partners can work together to produce the questions, or individual students can design the entire survey. A survey can be divided into sections so that some questions are group generated and others individually generated.

Surveys provide many opportunities to move SLIFE gradually from **oral transmission** to the **written word**. Teachers can begin with a totally or partially oral survey, accompanied by pictures or icons and with only a few questions. An original introductory survey, for instance, might look like this:

Who Likes to . . .?		
	Yes	No
cell phone		
MP3 player		
TV		
video game		

A survey such as this can easily be administered orally, with the pictures serving as memory prompts for the person gathering the information. Including the labels next to the picture reinforces the written form of the vocabulary items. After students ask each question, they can add a mark under the yes or no column. Once SLIFE become more comfortable using such surveys and extracting meaning from pictures, surveys can be administered primarily in written form.

Surveys provide ways for SLIFE to interact with each other, which helps to promote interconnectedness among students and with the teacher. As they discuss possible survey questions, and sequence them, students continually confer with one another. The topics themselves can be selected in such a way that they increase students' knowledge of each other. A personal opinion question can be included in each survey, such as, *What do you like best about our school?*

Such questions help SLIFE become more at ease in the school and build interconnectedness as they get to know different teachers and administrative staff, not only their own teachers. The question, which can also be asked of other students in the school, is immediately relevant as they are getting to know the school, their learning community, better each day.

To identify possible questions for the survey, students will use two main strategies. First, SLIFE consider their own information gaps. That is, how can they use the survey to find out more information about something to which they have already been exposed but about which they would like to expand their knowledge? In Mrs. McKeogh's unit on immigration, SLIFE learned about Jewish immigrants coming to the U.S. to escape pogroms in Eastern Europe and Russia. Since some of the SLIFE in the class were also refugees who had escaped persecution in their home country, the students decided to create questions related to persecution and immigration. One of their survey questions was: *Is there persecution in your country?*

The second strategy is for students to identify issues related to the topic of the survey on which respondents may have different points of view and create questions about these. Students can brainstorm to create questions about such an issue. In the issue question that follows, also relating to the study of immigration, the SLIFE wanted to see how others in their school felt about diversity, and they asked: *Do you like the diversity in American society?* For questions like this, the teacher may want to point out that such direct phrasing is likely to generate biased responses.

Types of Survey Questions

Survey questions can take many forms. An important distinction is between open-ended and closed-ended questions. In open-ended questions, the survey participants use their own words to respond, and answers may range from a paragraph or two to just a few words (Mertler, 2009). Open-ended questions allow participants the opportunity to construct a response freely. Such questions ask participants to contribute their own ideas to the survey topic, for example, or to give a viewpoint on a related issue not covered in the survey questions:

How do you like living here?

What do you like about our school? Why do you like this?

Open-ended questions, while interesting, may generate responses that SLIFE find cumbersome to sort out and may include complex language difficult for them to understand. Nevertheless, teachers may want to encourage the SLIFE to explore a particular topic by including some open-ended questions along with the closed-ended ones.

In closed-ended questions the responses are provided and the participants select among these responses (Mertler, 2009). For SLIFE, closed-ended questions are generally easier to analyze and report, as the responses fall into predicable patterns, both in terms of language and content. Closed-ended questions include five major types: numerical, categorical, multiple choice, scaled, and ranked.

Numerical

This is perhaps the most straightforward type of closed-ended question and is answered with a number:

How many years have you lived in the U.S.?

How many brothers do you have?

How many sisters do you have?

How old are you?

Categorical

In this case, the question presents participants with a set of alternatives, one of which fits them:

Are you male or female?

Are you

___ a student?
___ an administrator?
___ a teacher?
___ a staff member?
___ other?

Multiple Choice

For these questions, participants select one or more of the choices, depending on the instructions for the question.

Why did you leave your home country?

a. **religious reasons**

b. **economic reasons**

c. **political reasons**

d. **other** _____

Scaled

In scaled questions, participants must convey their attitudes or feelings by degree rather than by a yes/no choice. The most common of these is the Likert scale, in which participants indicate agreement or disagreement, on a five-point scale: strongly agree, agree, neutral (no opinion), disagree, and strongly disagree. For example, the earlier question about diversity could be rephrased as a scaled question:

Diversity is good for America.				
1	2	3	4	5
strongly disagree	disagree	no opinion	agree	strongly agree

Students can ask other types of attitude or feeling questions using a different scale that asks for information from participants other than the degree of their agreement or disagreement:

The food in the cafeteria is				
1	2	3	4	5
very bad	bad	okay	pretty good	excellent

Ranked

Rankings require the participant to take a series of items in a random order and put them into a meaningful order based on criteria provided in the survey. In a question on school subjects, participants could be asked to rank them numerically, depending on how well they like each subject:

Which subjects do you like? 1=favorite 4=least favorite

___ English

___ Math

___ Science

___ Social Studies

In all five types of closed-ended questions, the choices are supplied and the participant is offered very explicit options with respect to responding. These types of survey questions generate data that are easily quantifiable based on a tabulation of the results. Students can count the number of participants who selected each choice.

The teacher can start with surveys containing only one or two of these types. These are the very types of questions that these students commonly encounter in school but to which they have had little or no prior exposure. As the survey project is iterative, SLIFE have multiple opportunities to construct questions using these five question formats.

Using Preparation to Promote Skills

As students create questions, teachers can develop language and thinking skills in a number of ways. First, the very act of forming questions is a challenging task. Questions provide many opportunities for students to become familiar with and practice the different types of question formation. However, it is essential that teachers carefully scaffold question formation. For more specific information, we refer readers to the many ESL grammar texts on the market. DeCapua (2008), for example, is a one grammar text for teachers that provides detailed explanations and examples of all the different question formation patterns that all ELLs need to learn.

Next, the teacher can work with the students on ensuring that all questions are related to the chosen topic of the survey. Evaluating whether questions are relevant or irrelevant to a given topic is another academic task. Since the SLIFE are new to academic tasks, they may suggest questions that would be considered irrelevant from an academic viewpoint. For example, in the initial discussion of appropriate questions for the immigration survey, one student suggested asking, *Who do you live with?* Using the list of questions that the class has generated, the students consider carefully which ones really belong in the survey.

Third, surveys help to develop the concepts of objectivity and subjectivity. Distinguishing objective questions from subjective questions is an academic task. Objective questions ask participants for general knowledge or personal information. Subjective questions can be stated as choices, preferences, predictions, or any number of other perspectives on the topic. Surveys can ask for information or opinions, or include a combination of both types of questions.

Finally, surveys lend themselves to developing the academic task of sequencing. Once the students have decided on the final list of survey questions they need to be placed in some kind of logical order. It is important that there be some attention paid to the sequence and that the questions not be listed randomly. The students need to learn that general questions should come before specific ones based on the initial general question. A question such as "How many brothers and sisters do you have?" needs to come before "How old are they?" As teachers develop surveys with their SLIFE, they may find additional ways to use this type of project to build and enhance academic skills.

Step 3: Conduct the Survey

Once the SLIFE have created and sequenced the questions, it is time to prepare the survey instrument. This instrument can be administered in many forms. It can be oral or printed, presented nonverbally or verbally, hard copy or electronic, in English or in another language or in more than one language. This is one way that SLIFE can become creative and use their nonacademic and nonlinguistic abilities and backgrounds to generate an appealing interface for the participants.

Surveys that have been created as print documents are handed out to participants, who read the questions and enter their responses. For some surveys, teachers hand out the questions and collect them, just like a typical classroom exercise. For other surveys, students may pass out their questionnaires to other students not in their class; they may give them to teachers, school support staff, or community members. When students give out written surveys, they may need to be able to explain the directions and how the results will be used.

There are several ways oral surveys can be conducted. One possibility is to provide each participant with the written survey. The teacher or a student reads each question out loud as the participants read along and respond to the questions on the handout one by one. Another possibility for participants who are less comfortable with print is to provide only the response options on a handout while the questions are delivered orally. A third option is to conduct the survey completely orally. In this case, the participants hear the questions and respond orally while the person conducting the survey both asks the questions and records the responses. Or, the participant can provide oral responses as the questioner writes the answers.

In preparing an oral survey, careful attention must be given to how students will record the data to ensure later access. Students can record the responses on a digital recorder, onto the computer directly, or onto a response sheet. When using technology to record responses, it is important to test equipment to make sure it is functioning. Finally, there must be adequate wait time for the participants to respond before the next question is read. Regardless of how questions are posed and responses collected, under the MALP instructional model, it is essential that students have opportunities to combine oral transmission with the written word.

This sample survey produced by Mr. Patek's SLIFE shows a variety of question types and demonstrates the wide range of possibilities for class surveys.

Survey about School Subjects

Name _____

Date _____

1. Which subjects do you like? Please rate them on a scale from 1 to 4.
    1= favorite 4=least favorite.

    ___ Math

    ___ Science

    ___ Social Studies

    ___ English

2. Please tell why you chose your subject for #1.

3. My teacher in my favorite subject is

1	2	3	4	5
excellent	very good	good	okay	not good

4. My teacher in my *least* favorite subject is

1	2	3	4	5
excellent	very good	good	okay	not good

Step 4: Analyze and Quantify the Results

This next step consists of data analysis—a key academic task that includes many of the types of academic thinking, such as comparison and contrast, discovering relationships, categorization, and classification. For SLIFE to be successful in this task, the process requires careful scaffolding. As SLIFE analyze the survey, they consult with one another to help each other and to compare their findings. The language and content pertaining to the survey are familiar to them because they created the questions themselves. Even when some responses, such as open-ended question responses, contain unfamiliar language and content, SLIFE are likely to be able to use the context to interpret them.

Before engaging in an analysis of the survey results, the students need to review all of the responses carefully. If the questions are all closed-ended, this is straightforward. If there are open-ended questions, they will need to be read closely with a view to finding a way to interpret or categorize them.

Once the students have reviewed all of the responses, they need to tabulate them. First, they need to see how many total responses they have for each question. Next, for each question they count the number of respondents who selected each of the possible answers and record these on a chart. Finally, they express these counts as percentages or fractions of the total. In this example, the students have done this for one question. Note that the percentages add up to 100%.

Sample Immigration Survey Data	
Question	**For what reason did you leave your country?**
Results	55% of the students left their countries for economic reasons.
	23% of the students left their countries for political reasons.
	22% of the students left their countries to join their family.

Using the information in this example, Mrs. McKeogh's SLIFE wrote *More students left their country for economic reasons than for political reasons*. To help SLIFE in their analysis of data, she provided these sentence frames.

1. _____ percent of the students left their country for _____ reasons.

2. _____ students left their country for _____ reasons than for _____ reasons.

After SLIFE have examined and analyzed the data, the way that they choose to represent the analysis visually can vary. SLIFE can learn to show their analyses graphically with pie charts, bar graphs, and other such representations of data, which become part of their report on the survey data.

Step 5: Draw Conclusions

Using survey data is effective in helping SLIFE learn to draw conclusions, an important academic task. Since by now all the language and content are familiar to the students, teachers can focus on what it means to draw a conclusion from data. In drawing conclusions, the students learn to observe patterns or trends that emerge from the responses. To further develop their academic thinking, students should think about what they learned from the survey about this topic, and how specific questions helped them to get a better understanding of the topic, either in terms of facts, opinions, or both. Looking back at the example from Mrs. McKeogh's class SLIFE were able to come up with this conclusion: *So, most students left their country for economic reasons.*

Step 6: Report on the Survey

The next step requires the students to present the results to the class and discuss them, followed by some type of dissemination. The reporting phase mirrors many other such class activities in which presentations are made. In these final two steps of the survey project, the class as a whole will be able to process the material from the survey and focus on the new language and content that may have been generated from it.

As we continually emphasize, sentence frames are an effective way to guide SLIFE in sentence formation. Using teacher-generated sentence frames for reporting results gives SLIFE several ways to present the data they have collected. With such scaffolding, the students can focus on the data they are presenting and yet at the same time build their skills in using the academic language required for school projects.

1. The results show us that _____.

2. Of the _____ (number) people in this survey _____ (number) responded _____ and _____ (number) responded _____.

3. _____ (number) students like _____ (name of subject) better than _____ (name of subject).

4. _____(number) students like _____ (name of subject) the best.

5. (number) students like _____ (name of subject) the least.

Note that the students practiced using the comparative and superlative structures *better, the best,* and *the least.* There are many possibilities for students to practice different types of structures in reporting their results.

The class presentation can take many forms. Students can present the results orally or in writing or both. They can use a presentation application, such as Power-Point, or they can create a poster or mural. The length and complexity of the report will depend on the abilities of the students, but the content of the report is the data. These data have been tabulated, the patterns that emerged examined, and conclusions drawn. Taken together, the results will demonstrate that the students succeeded both in designing a survey to obtain usable data and in analyzing that data correctly.

Either during the presentation or following it, all students discuss the survey. The class discussion focuses on the results and the new understanding of the topic, or new perspectives on the topic, that were gained from the survey. One or more of the students can take notes on this discussion and add them to the survey report.

As SLIFE hear and/or read the results of the survey, regardless of their individual roles within the survey project, they share the experience of an activity in which the entire class has had a role, bringing them closer and building community in the classroom.

Step 7: Disseminate the Results

The culminating activity in the survey project is to show the results of the survey to a larger audience and/or to put them into a lasting format of some kind. In displaying or publishing their work, the students reproduce the material from the survey and revisit it, as in a formal written presentation. The most immediate way to do this is the display. This can be as simple as creating a wall poster with the survey results that goes up in the room and can be referred to later as a resource to guide future survey reports and to provide content on the topic of the survey. Another option is to have a bulletin board in a school hallway designated for the surveys and to add them as the year goes along, perhaps with other materials from other MALP projects. Publishing, as in a newsletter, while less immediate than the display, permits a wider audience.

After the Survey—Following Up

At the conclusion of the project, students share their thoughts about what they learned from going through the survey process. Each time the class undertakes a survey project, students may find that they have gained additional knowledge and skills that will transfer to their other school tasks. For example, much of the material in subject area classes and textbooks presents data in the same formats as discussed in this chapter. If students have themselves participated in creating such data displays and explaining them to others, they are more likely to understand them and work on interpreting them rather than pass them by or leave it up to others to do the analysis.

It should now be evident how the application of MALP through the survey project helps SLIFE make the learning paradigm shift. A class survey includes all three components of MALP: it accepts the two SLIFE conditions for learning, makes transitions to individual accountability and the written word comfortably, and incorporates academic tasks. Moreover, in this project, students see from start to finish an important characteristic of academic work, the schemata of investigation, analysis, conclusions, and dissemination. After being participants in the entire process, they will be more able to relate to what is presented in their textbooks, by their teachers, and eventually, when they conduct their own research projects, by their fellow students. The skills SLIFE gain, the academic language they develop, and the academic ways of thinking in which they engage, are all facilitated by the mutually adaptive approach. With MALP as a framework, teachers of SLIFE have a structure they can use to make students comfortable with formal classroom learning; using class surveys is an excellent place to begin.

For Further Exploration

1. Not everyone may feel comfortable with surveys. Imagine that you have just finished introducing the idea of surveys and discussed doing a class survey with your SLIFE. One of the students has not participated very much and looks unhappy. You spend a few minutes alone with him and realize that he feels very uncomfortable asking people questions and thinks it rude. How might you address his feelings while encouraging him to participate in the survey project? What accommodations or modifications can you suggest?

2. Properly implemented, a survey project will include the three components and six elements of MALP. Since a survey is an ongoing project that takes place over the course of several days, even weeks, not all components and elements will be included in every lesson. Nevertheless, over the course of a survey, the different elements will all need to be incorporated at some point. To illustrate this point:

   a. Make a copy of the MALP Checklist, Figure 4.1.

   b. Reread this chapter.

   c. As you read, try to fill out the MALP Checklist with the information provided in the chapter about conducting surveys. You may want to refer back to Chapter 4 and the discussion of the MALP Checklist.

   d. After you finish, discuss the following questions with a partner or in small groups:

      - Were you able to provide at least one answer for each of the six questions?

      - Was it easy? Difficult? Explain.

      - Which elements of MALP did you see occurring more often? Less often? Why do you think this is so?

      - What additional elaboration of the seven steps can you suggest?

3. Do an Internet search for ESL Surveys, and find one you could adapt for a SLIFE class survey. Then bring in this survey and share how you would adapt it to make it more appropriate for this population.

4. Using The 7 Steps in a Survey Project on page 115 and Mr. Patek's sample survey, design a survey activity for your class. Use the MALP Checklist to be sure you are implementing all elements of MALP in different steps of the project.

8

Reflecting on MALP

WE HAVE ELUCIDATED A NEW INSTRUCTIONAL MODEL, MALP, and examined the balancing of language, content, and culture in addressing the needs of SLIFE in this book.

As they adapt to formal education, there are certain things SLIFE must learn—notably, to regard and use print as a primary resource for information and as a vehicle for communication, and to be individually accountable for their work. The best way to transition them is to incorporate their preferred ways, oral transmission and shared responsibility, into our teaching and gradually accustom them to the ways of U.S. schools. MALP transitions the students to print—not just by teaching and rehearsing the basics of literacy, but by making strong connections between oral transmission and the written word. In addition, and perhaps most important for their ultimate success, because SLIFE are unfamiliar with academic ways of thinking, teachers must provide them with extensive opportunities to learn and to practice via academic tasks that use familiar language and content, allowing SLIFE to focus on the task itself and not be distracted by other unfamiliar elements. It is this third component of MALP that requires an understanding of the balancing of the three schemata: linguistic, content, and formal, so that teachers can plan activities to focus exclusively on the new formal schemata.

Ms. Kempinski Makes the Journey

Despite the realities facing them regarding curriculum, placement of students, and standardized testing requirements, teachers of SLIFE are choosing to implement MALP and are finding that the investment in adapting their teaching is worthwhile when they look at the results in terms of student motivation and accomplishment (DeCapua & Marshall, 2010b; Marshall, DeCapua, & Antolini, 2010). One such teacher is Ms. Kempinski, who transformed her teaching after professional development training in MALP. When we first met Ms. Kempinski, she was faced with a high school math class of 20 beginner ELLs, all of whom had been identified as SLIFE. Ms. Kempinski was mandated to teach this class of SLIFE Integrated Algebra, yet most of them were still struggling with basic operations.

In her other math classes, Ms. Kempinski taught with very positive results; however, in this particular class, she asked for assistance in the form of professional development. Her main concern was content and, to a lesser extent, language. In our initial meeting with her, she expressed her general frustrations:

> *Some come late. If they are on time they don't bring a pencil, the majority don't do homework, and I can't get them to listen to me regarding their behavior. How can I help them be successful if the basics are not there?*

Let us take a look at one of the early lessons we observed. We enter the classroom and see the chairs in rows and on the wall a commercially made poster encouraging students to do their homework. Students drift in slowly and wait at their desks until Ms. Kempinski reminds them to look at the math problems on the board and begin their work. This lesson, like all her lessons, begins with an activity called Do Now, followed by a presentation on the lesson topic for the day, practice problems, and finally, a homework assignment. This scripted approach is the one uniformly implemented in her large urban high school.

For the Do Now portion of the lesson, Ms. Kempinski begins with three problems from the previous lesson written on the board. The class has just started to discuss the rules for the order in which to solve mathematical problems, known as the Order of Operations principle. The students complete the problems on their own at their desks. When the allotted time is up, Ms. Kempinski reviews each problem by calling on an individual student to tell her the answer or write the answer on the board. She follows this activity with a lecture presentation on a new type of math problem they will learn today. As she lectures, she demonstrates how to complete the new problems using examples that she writes on the board. The new problems still focus on the Order of Operations but are more difficult than the previous ones, as these involve additional, more complex operations. She instructs the students to copy what she writes on the board into their notebooks. After she has explained and demonstrated this new type of problem, Ms. Kempinski does three additional ones, calling on individual students to volunteer as the class goes through the problems together on the board, step by step. There is virtually no time for questions and answers as there barely is time to go through the problems, given that she must allot a specific amount of time each day for students to practice solving problems individually.

Once the class has completed the three additional problems on the board together, Ms. Kempinski hands out a worksheet and instructs the students that they have until the end of the period to practice similar problems on their own. While they are working alone on their worksheets, she circulates around the room to help those who raise their hands for help, reviewing again individually how to solve the problems. When students have completed their worksheets and Ms. Kempinski has checked their work, she selects students to go to the board to put up one of the practice problems for the rest of the class to see. Ms. Kempinski reminds the students to check the board to see if they solved the problems correctly and to copy anything they missed into their math notebooks to help them do the homework they will have for tomorrow's class. At the end of class, Ms. Kempinski hands out another worksheet with similar problems for the students to complete as their homework assignment.

Our first impression was that Ms. Kempinski was a very knowledgeable and very organized teacher. Her lesson moved along efficiently, and she was intent on presenting the material as clearly as possible. It also struck us immediately that this was a very teacher-centered classroom, with minimal student input. Although she tried to help each student individually as they struggled to complete the worksheet, Ms. Kempinski had not allowed for peer interaction and support, had not made direct connections between oral and written modes, and had not made explicit new academic ways of thinking—pedagogical considerations very important for SLIFE.

We now enter Ms. Kempinski classroom several months later, after she has participated in MALP-based professional development training. Today, we immediately see a learning community. There is a monthly calendar hanging showing birthdays, holidays, and key assignment dates. The walls display completed student projects. The board lists the three objectives for the lesson, along with a chart of sentence frames as a guide for the students. Before beginning the lesson, Ms. Kempinski has referred to her binder containing notes about each student, along with that student's math issues as they relate to the current work in the unit. She pairs the students based on what they can do for each other in terms of math, language, or both.

In this new unit the class is going to be introduced to "like terms" and "unlike terms" to see what the criteria are for differentiating them. In mathematics, a "term" is any number (3), variable (x), or combination (3xy), with or without an exponent ($3x^2$). This concept relates to comparison and contrast, the key academic task upon which Ms. Kempinski will focus. She asks them to practice by listing some ways that they, as individuals, are similar to or different from each other. After this, she points out that they can select the criteria they want to use—native language, native country, height, number of people in the family, and so on. She then points out that in math, by contrast, there are set criteria that must be used to decide if two mathematical terms are alike or not.

She is now ready to introduce the math concept of like and unlike terms. Ms. Kempinski focuses on the word *term*. As she says each part of the term and points to it, she labels each part of a sample term: *coefficient, variable, exponent*. She calls attention to why it is important to know if two terms are alike by asking, "Can we add them together or 'combine' them?"

Ms. Kempinski also addresses the issue of what parts of the term matter, referring back to the concept of *set criteria* she had reviewed previously. Because, in previous lessons, Ms. Kempinski has carefully scaffolded the several parts of a mathematical term, that is, the coefficient, the variable, and the exponent, and provided sentence frames for them to use in responding to the examples, the students are able to focus on the new concept—like and unlike terms.

Each pair of students produces a poster for the unit, using a template Ms. Kempinski has supplied. The students provide their own examples of like and unlike terms. She gives each pair terms to analyze and the criteria they are to use to determine the placement of a term in that category. On their posters, they must include their responses to three items: (A) Are they like terms? (B) Tell how you know. and (C) Combine or rewrite the expression. For Item B, they need be able to state the criteria they used to decide if the terms were like or unlike; that is, whether they have the same variable and the same exponent or not. The groups present their posters to each other, which then go up on the wall for reference. In this lesson on like and unlike terms, students were able to manage the new concept of combining only like terms because she had focused earlier on basic and essential mathematical terminology—*coefficient, variable, exponent*. While most of Ms. Kempinski's fellow math teachers assumed that students would be familiar with this vocabulary by the time they were in high school, she did not assume any prior knowledge and ensured she introduced everything, knowing that almost everything was a totally new concept for SLIFE.

Ms. Kempinski has incorporated the main points from this book into her teaching. She uses the three components of MALP: (A) accept the conditions; (B) combine the processes; and (C) focus on new activities for learning. Her classroom is now a project-based learning one. Reflecting on her most challenging class, Ms. Kempinski tells us:

> This is my new favorite class—we really have a good time and they actually get it! It makes such as difference to teach this way. For SLIFE who were failing, I can see real progress; they still take longer than other ELLs to catch on, but they are trying and succeeding over time. I now have a 60 percent pass rate in that class, up from only 20 percent before.

In working with teachers of SLIFE on lessons and projects, such as those presented in this text, we have found multiple benefits from using the MALP Checklist. As they carefully review the MALP instructional model, teachers must identify specific aspects of their teaching that incorporate each of the six elements. This, in turn, ensures that they are infusing all the elements of MALP into their lessons. The lesson and project analysis they conduct with the MALP Checklist reinforces their understanding that the elements, when implemented together, result in promoting a positive learning experience for SLIFE. Ms. Kempinski's consistent use of the MALP Checklist in preparing her lessons helped her ensure that she indeed incorporated the three components and six elements regularly, reducing the cultural dissonance of the students and better preparing them for learning.

Revisiting Cultural Dissonance

The introduction presented a chart of what teachers and learners in U.S. mainstream classrooms assume about the goals of K–12 instruction and what the learner brings to the classroom. In Chapters 1–7, we have explored each of these assumptions, how they differ for SLIFE, and how teachers can transition them to the U.S. classroom.

As we have emphasized, MALP is an instructional model that calls for adaptation on the parts of both the teachers and SLIFE to reduce the cultural dissonance these students encounter. Although we have focused largely on how the teacher must adjust and adapt as an instructor to implement MALP, it is, of course, also vital for SLIFE to adjust and adapt. They must transition to feeling comfortable with, and becoming accustomed to, print as a primary resource, individual accountability, and academic ways of thinking.

Figure 8.1 shows two divergent perspectives on SLIFE with respect to their experiences in U.S. schools. The right end of the continuum represents the formal educational learning paradigm. The left end represents the informal learning paradigm of SLIFE. The center of the continuum illustrates where SLIFE are in secondary schools today. The deficit perspective is illustrated by Arrow #1 pointing back to the left. In this view, SLIFE are seen as sharing the assumptions about education and the learning paradigm of the U.S. educational system but failing to achieve success. However, the SLIFE do not approach education from the right end, which is unfamiliar to them. Rather, most SLIFE in U.S. schools begin at the left end of the continuum, where, as members of collectivistic cultures who have little or no formal education, they have to move toward the other end, toward an individualistic culture and academic ways of thinking, when they find themselves in U.S. secondary schools. This perspective is illustrated by Arrow #2, showing SLIFE as bringing their familiar learning paradigm with them as they move along the continuum of ways of learning. Far from being deficient learners, these students have simply been accustomed to a very different way of learning. They have actually made credible attempts to move along the continuum to the right despite the challenges they face.

The continuum emphasizes that SLIFE have their own set of assumptions about teaching and learning. Yet, neither U.S. mainstream teachers nor SLIFE necessarily realize that (a) they have these assumptions and that (b) the assumptions each group has are very different. MALP makes these different assumptions explicit, views teaching and learning on a cultural continuum, and offers a mutually adaptive approach that meets SLIFE halfway and helps transition them to the right side of the continuum. For these students, MALP offers a pathway to success. It is essential that U.S. educators see SLIFE as students who are coming from a different end of the continuum with a very different paradigm and who are moving *toward* our system. SLIFE, in addition to academic issues, are confronting cultural issues of learning.

FIGURE 8.1   Ways of Learning Continuum

Informal Learning   U.S. Formal Education

'familiar to SLIFE'   SLIFE in U.S. Schools   'unfamiliar to SLIFE'

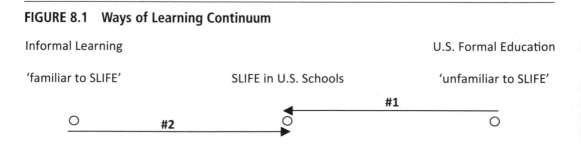

We now look at Vuong, a student who has, like Ms. Kempinski, made a journey. In this case, the journey took him along the continuum of the ways of learning toward the U.S. paradigm and academic success.

Vuong Makes the Journey

Education Is Just the Beginning . . .

We first met Vuong in Chapter 1 when we read the first lines of his journal excerpt describing his first experiences with print (see page 24). The son of a fisherman in Vietnam, Vuong came to this country as a teenager. Although he had had little formal schooling, he was placed into high school based on his age. Through his participation in content-area classes infused with MALP, he became successful over time, and eventually completed a two-year degree in Automotive Technology.

We close with Vuong's voice, beginning with the complete version of his journal excerpt, the first paragraph of which we saw in Chapter 1:

> *"The most importants I have learned about the United States that is a book, newspapers, or notebook and pens. These things are always let me know how to live here.*
>
> *I can remember once upon a time, that the first time I came here and I didn't know anything about the United States. At that time, I just pick up the textbooks from my teacher, and then I read it, but I didn't understand it much because I didn't study English before, at that times I picked up a dictionary to look up the words I didn't understand and translate by my native language . . .*
>
> *. . . I always remember the books are the most important things for me to learn when I live in the United States."*

It is important to note that had Vuong been left to decipher the U.S. educational system on his own, he may have appeared to be learning but may not have truly shifted his paradigm. He benefited, however, from instructors trained in MALP who helped him move along the continuum of ways of learning.

Here is a page from Vuong's ESL journal, two years later, after extensive instruction in sheltered courses using MALP. Vuong produced this piece, again reflecting on his learning in the United States. MALP allowed him to gain insight into his new language, his new culture, and, in particular, his new future. He gave it the heading *Poemtry*.

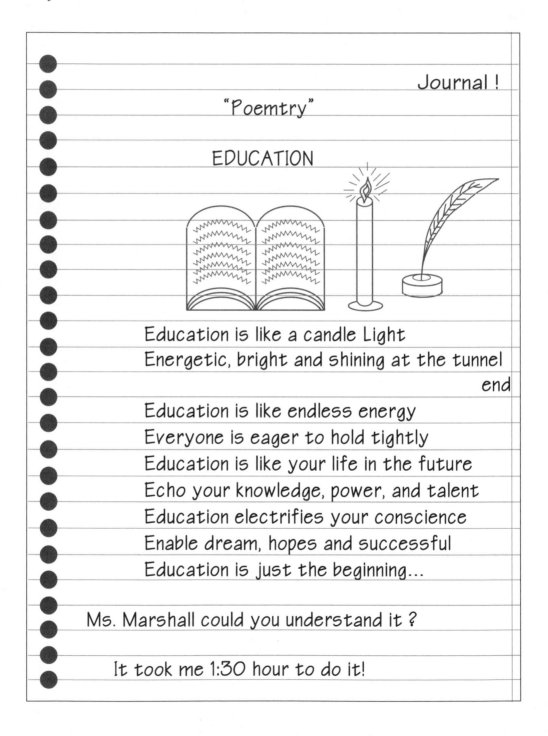

Journal !

"Poemtry"

EDUCATION

Education is like a candle Light
Energetic, bright and shining at the tunnel
                                          end
Education is like endless energy
Everyone is eager to hold tightly
Education is like your life in the future
Echo your knowledge, power, and talent
Education electrifies your conscience
Enable dream, hopes and successful
Education is just the beginning...

Ms. Marshall could you understand it ?

It took me 1:30 hour to do it!

For Further Exploration

1. As for any major shift in pedagogical orientation, sustained efforts must be made and supported, and positive results demonstrated in order for innovations to take hold. Ms. Kempinski's department chair provided administrative support, allowing her to restructure her lesson plans, have alternative seating arrangements, and take more time to build concepts.

    a. What issues and/or obstacles do you believe might prevent teachers from implementing MALP in your school?

    b. How could you address these issues and gain support for the MALP instructional model? Reflect on what you have learned from this text as support.

2. While we began to develop this model as we sat in classrooms watching and listening—seeing SLIFE as disengaged learners, their potential not realized—we have come to believe that the model has possibilities for other learners as well. If we return to our notion of a continuum of ways of learning presented in this chapter, we can imagine that there are other students who are perhaps not as obviously experiencing cultural dissonance, but who also find themselves uncomfortable with the U.S. high school classroom experience. Think of other students you know who are not SLIFE but who are also struggling learners.

    a. Where would you place them on the continuum? Explain.

    b. Do you think they could benefit from an approach based on the MALP instructional model? Why or why not?

3. Teachers often tell us that they have SLIFE who are not ELLs but speakers of English dialects or creoles, such as Jamaicans or Guyanese. They wonder whether these students, too, might benefit from MALP. Consider what you have learned in this book.

    a. How could MALP help English-speaking SLIFE? Be specific and provide examples.

    b. What adjustments would you make if you were using MALP for this population?

    c. Using a lesson you have taught or have seen taught, explain how you would incorporate MALP for these SLIFE.

4. The overrepresentation of ELLs in special education has been a concern for some time (Coutinho & Oswald, 2006). These concerns are even more applicable to SLIFE since they are difficult to diagnose because of additional factors such as their low or no literacy skills and/or low grade–appropriate content-area knowledge (DeCapua, Smathers, & Tang, 2009).

   a. In your experience, what are some of the issues in trying to determine if a SLIFE might need special education? Interview other ESL teachers and guidance counselors to get their perspectives on referrals of ELLs and SLIFE to special education.

   b. If you have a class of SLIFE that includes students with Individualized Educational Plans (IEPs), take notes on how they respond as you implement MALP in your classroom. Identify aspects of MALP that may assist in shedding light on the overrepresentation of SLIFE in special education.

5. Reread the poem by Vuong. Reconsider his journal entry from two years earlier. How do these two writing samples reflect the paradigm shift for this student? Cite examples from the text to illustrate specific ways in which the student has embraced the U.S. learning paradigm. Notice not only language and content, which are themselves quite relevant, but also the type of thinking Vuong is doing as he composes his piece.

6. Consider the note that Vuong wrote below his poem.

   Teacher, could you understand it?
   It took me 1:30 to do it!

Revisit his two pieces of writing, and think about why he included the note, what he was trying to convey by it, and how it further illustrates that he has made the journey to formal education successfully.

References

Aronson, E. (1978). *The Jigsaw classroom*. Beverly Hills, CA: Sage.

Abedi, J., Hofstetter, C., & Lord, C. (2004). Assessment accommodations for English language learners: Implications for policy-based empirical research. *Review of Educational Research, 7*, 1–28.

Abrami, P., Poulsen, C., & Chambers, B. (2004). Teacher motivation to implement an educational innovation: Factors differentiating users and non-users of cooperative learning. *Educational Psychology, 24*, 201–216.

Alderson, J. C. (2000). *Assessing reading*. Cambridge, U.K.: Cambridge University Press.

Alexander, P., Kulikowich, J., & Schulze, S. (1994). How subject matter knowledge affects recall and interest. *American Educational Research Journal, 31*, 313–337.

Alexander, R. (2000). Culture and pedagogy: International comparisons in primary education. Malden, MA: Blackwell.

Althen, G. (2002). *American ways: A guide for foreigners in the United States*. Boston: Intercultural Press.

Anderson, L. W. (Ed.), Krathwohl, D. R., (Ed.), Airasian, P., Cruikshank, K., Mayer, R., Pintrich, P., Raths, J., & Wittrock, M. (2001). *A taxonomy for learning, teaching, and assessing: A revision of Bloom's Taxonomy of Educational Objectives* (Complete Edition). White Plains, NY: Longman.

Anderson, N. J. (1999). *Exploring second language reading*. Boston: Heinle & Heinle.

Angelo, T. A., & Cass, K. P. (1993). *A handbook of classroom assessment techniques for college teachers*. San Francisco: Jossey-Bass.

August, A., Goldenberg, C., & Rueda, R. (2006). Native American children and youth: Culture, language, and literacy. *Journal of American Indian Education, 35*, 24–37.

Barron, B., Schwartz, D., Vye, N., Moore, A., Petrosino, A., Zech, L., Bransford, J., & The Cognition and Technology Group at Vanderbilt. (1998). Doing with understanding: Lessons from research on problem and project-based learning. *The Journal of the Learning Sciences, 7*, 271–311.

Bassey, M. (1999). *Western education and political domination in Africa*. Westport, CT: Bergin and Garvey.

Biemiller, A. (2005). Vocabulary development and instruction: A prerequisite for school learning. In D. Dickinson & S. Neuman (Eds.), *Handbook of early literacy research, Vol. 3.* (pp. 503–523). Mahwah, NJ: Lawrence Erlbaum.

Bifuh-Ambe, E. (2009). Literacy skills acquisition and use: A study of an English language learner in a U.S. university context. *Adult Basic Education and Literacy Journal, 3*, 24–33.

Bloom, B. (1956). *Taxonomy of educational objectives, Handbook I: The cognitive domain*. New York: David McKay.

Bradford, M. (2005). Motivating students through project-based service learning. *T.H.E. Journal, 32*, 29–30.

Brown, D. (2003). Urban teachers' use of culturally responsive management strategies. *Theory into Practice, 42*, 277–282.

Browning-Aiken, A. (2005). Border crossings: Funds of knowledge within an immigrant household. In N. Gonzalez, L. Moll,, & C. Amanti (Eds.), *Funds of knowledge: Theorizing practices in households, communities, and classrooms* (pp. 167–181). Mahwah, NJ: Lawrence Erlbaum.

Cantoni-Harvey, G. (1987). *Content-area language instruction: Approaches and strategies*. Reading, MA: Addison-Wesley.

Carr, T., & Jitendra, A. (2000). Using hypermedia and multimedia to promote project-based learning of at-risk high school students. *Intervention in School and Clinic, 36,* 40–44.

Carrell, P. (1998). Some causes of text-boundedness and schema interference. In P., Carrell, J. Devine, & D. Eskey (Eds.), *Interactive approaches to second language reading* (pp. 101–113). Cambridge, MA: Cambridge University Press.

Carrier, K. (2005). Supporting science learning through science literacy objectives for English language learners. *Science Activities: Classroom Projects and Curriculum Ideas, 42,* 5–11.

Cauce, A. M., & Domenech-Rodríguez, M. (2002). Latino families: Myths and realities. In J. Contreras, A. Neal-Barnett, & K. Kerns (Eds.), *Latino children and families in the United States: Current research and future directions* (pp. 3–26). Westport, CT: Praeger.

Cavazos, A. (2009). Reflections of a Latina student-teacher: Refusing low expectations for Latina/o students. *American Secondary Education, 37,* 70–79.

Cazden, C. (1988). *Classroom discourse: The language of teaching and learning.* Portsmouth, NH: Heinemann.

Cazden, C. (2001). *Classroom discourse: The language of teaching and learning* (2nd ed.). Portsmouth, NH: Heinemann.

Chavajay, P., & Rogoff, B. (2002). Schooling and traditional collaborative social organization of problem solving by Mayan mothers and children. *Developmental Psychology, 38,* 55–66.

Clarke, M. (2006). *A place to stand: Essays for educators in troubled times.* Ann Arbor: University of Michigan Press.

Clarke, M. (2007). *Common ground, contested territory: Examining roles of English language teachers in troubled times.* Ann Arbor: University of Michigan Press.

Clarke, M., Davis, A., Rhodes, L., & Baker, E. (1996). Creating coherence: High achieving classrooms for minority students. Final report of research conducted under U.S. Department of Education, Field Initiated Studies Program, grant R117 E302 44. Denver: University of Colorado.

Cohen, E. (1994). *Designing groupwork: Strategies for the heterogeneous classroom.* (2nd ed.). New York: Teachers College Press.

Cohen, J. (2009). Using student-generated surveys. *Essential Teacher, 7,* 42–44.

Cole, M. (1998). Can cultural psychology help us think about diversity? *Mind, Culture, and Activity, 5,* 291–304.

Colombo, M. (2002). English language literacy: Motivating culturally diverse students to improve reading and writing skills. *The New England Reading Association Journal, 38,* 10–14.

Commeyras, M., & Inyega, H. (2007). An integrative review of teaching reading in Kenyan primary schools. *Reading Research Quarterly, 42,* 258–281.

Constantino, R., & Lavadenz, M. (1993). Newcomer schools: First impressions. *Peabody Journal of Education, 69,* 82–101.

Corbett, D., Wilson, B., & Williams, B. (2002). *Effort and excellence in urban classrooms: Expecting and getting success with all students.* New York: Teachers College Press.

Coutinho, M., & Oswald, D. (2006). *Disproportionate representation of culturally and linguistically diverse students in special education: Measuring the problem.* Students in Special Education Brief. U.S. Department of Education. http:www.nccrest.org/Briefs/Students_in_SPED_Brief.pdf

Cuellar, I., Arnold, B., & Gonzalez, G. (1995). Cognitive referents of acculturation: Assesssment of cultural constructs in Mexican Americans. *Journal of Community Psychology, 23,* 339–356.

Cummins, J. (1984). *Bilingual education and special education: Issues in assessment and pedagogy.* San Diego, CA: College Hill.

Cummins, J., Brown, K., & Sayers, D. (2007). *Literacy, technology, and diversity: Teaching for success in changing times.* Boston: Pearson.

DeCapua, A. (2008). *Grammar for teachers: A guide to American English for native and non-native speakers.* Boston: Springer.

DeCapua A., & Marshall, H.W. (2010a). Limited formally schooled English language learners in U.S. classrooms, *Urban Review, 42,* 159–173.

DeCapua, A., & Marshall, H.W. (2010b). Serving ELLs with limited or interrupted education: Intervention that works, *TESOL Journal, 1,* 49–70.

DeCapua, A., & Marshall, H.W. (2011). Reaching ELLs at risk: Instruction for students with limited/interrupted formal education succeed, *Preventing School Failure,* doi:10.1080/ 10459880903291680.

DeCapua A., & McDonell, T. (2008). There is more to an iceberg than the tip: Culture and second language writing in the classroom. In J. Paull (Ed.), *From Hip Hop to Hyperlinks: Practical Approaches for Teaching Culture in the Composition Classroom* (pp. 136–148). Cambridge, U.K.: Cambridge Scholars Publications.

DeCapua, A., Smathers, W., & Tang, F. (2009). *Meeting the needs of students with limited or interrupted schooling: A guide for educators.* Ann Arbor: University of Michigan Press.

DeCapua, A., Smathers, W., & Tang, F. (2007). Addressing the challenges and needs of students with interrupted formal education (SIFE). *Educational Policy & Leadership, 65,* 40–46.

DeCapua, A., & Wintergerst, A. (2004). *Crossing cultures in the language classroom.* Ann Arbor: University of Michigan Press.

De Jesús, A., & Antrop-González, R. (2006). Instrumental relationships and high expectations: Exploring critical care in two Latino community-based schools. *Intercultural Education, 17,* 281–299.

DeKeyser, P. (2007). (Ed.). *Practice in a second language: Perspectives from applied linguistics and cognitive psychology.* New York: Cambridge University Press.

Delgado-Gaitan, C. (2004). *Involving Latino families in schools: Raising student achievement through home-school partnerships.* Thousand Oaks, CA: Corwin Press.

Delgado-Gaitan, C., & Trueba, H. (1991). *Crossing cultural borders: Education for immigrant families in America.* Bristol, PA: Falmer Press.

Denny, J. P. (1991). Rational thought in oral culture and literate decontexualization. In D. Olson & N. Torrance (Eds.), *Literacy and orality* (pp. 66–89). New York: Cambridge University Press.

Dörnyei, Z. (2002). The motivational basis of language learning tasks. In P. Robinson (Ed.), *Individual differences and instructed language learning* (pp. 137–158). Amsterdam: John Benjamins.

Echevarria, M. (2003). Anomalies as a catalyst for middle school students' knowledge construction and scientific reasoning during science inquiry, *Journal of Educational Psychology, 95,* 357–374.

Echevarria, J., & Graves, A. (2007). *Sheltered content instruction: Teaching English language learners with diverse abilities* (3rd ed). Boston: Allyn & Bacon.

Echevarria, J., Vogt, M.E., & Short, D. (2008). *Making content comprehensible for English Language Learners: The SIOP model* (3rd ed.). Boston: Allyn & Bacon.

Falicov, C. J. (1998). *Latino families in therapy: A guide to multicultural practice.* New York: Guilford.

Ferretti, R. , MacArthur, C., & Okolo, C. (2001). Teaching for historical understanding in inclusive classrooms. *Learning Disability Quarterly, 24,* 59–71.

Ferris, D., & Hedgecock, J. (1998). *Teaching ESL composition: Purpose, process, and practice.* Mahwah, NJ: Lawrence Erlbaum.

Flynn, J. (2007). *What is intelligence?* New York: Cambridge University Press.

Forestal, P. (1990). Talking: Toward classroom action. In M. Brubacher, R. Payne, & K. Rickett (Eds.), *Perspectives on small group learning: Theory and practice* (pp. 159–173). Oakville, ON: Rubicon.

Foster, P., & Ohta, A. (2005). Negotiation for meaning and peer assistance in second language classrooms. *Applied Linguistics, 26,* 402–430.

Freeman, Y., & Freeman, S. (2002). *Closing the achievement gap: How to reach limited-formal-schooling and long-term English learners:* Portsmouth, NH: Heinemann.

Freire, P. (1994). *Pedagogy of hope.* New York: Continuum.

Fry, R. (2005). *The higher dropout rate of foreign-born teens: The role of schooling abroad.* Washington, DC: Pew Hispanic Center.

Fugundes, F. (2007). Charles Reis Felix's "Through a Portagee Gate"; Lives parceled out in stories. *MELUS, 32,* 151–163.

Fuligini, A., Tseng, V., & Lam, M. (1999). Attitudes toward family obligations among American adolescents with Asian, Latin American, and European backgrounds. *Child Development, 70,* 1030–1044.

Gallegos, M. (2005). La educacíon en Latinoamérica y El caribe: Puntos críticos y utopias. *Revista Latinoamericana de Estudios Educativos, 35,* 7–34.

Gardner, W., Gabriel, S., & Lee, A. Y. (1999). "I" value freedom, but "we" value relationships: Self-construal priming mirrors cultural differences in judgment. *Psychological Science, 10,* 321–326.

Gass, S., & Mackey, A. (2006). Input, interaction, and output in second language acquisition. In B. VanPatten & J. Williams (Eds.), *Theories in second language acquisition* (pp. 175–196). New York: Routledge.

Gay, G. (2000). *Culturally responsive teaching: Theory, research, and practice.* New York: Teachers College Press.

Gee, J. (1996). *Social linguistics and literacies: Ideology in discourses* (2nd ed.). London: Taylor and Francis.

Gehrke, M. E. (1998). Home, school, community partnerships. In J. M. Allen (Ed.), *School counseling: New perspectives & practices* (pp. 122–126). Greensboro, NC: ERIC Clearinghouse on Counseling and Student Services.

Gibbons, P. (2002). *Scaffolding language, scaffolding learning: Teaching second language learners in the mainstream classroom.* Portsmouth, NH: Heinemann.

Goldenberg, C. (2008). Teaching English language learners: What the research does and does not say. *American Educator, Summer,* 8–44.

González, N., Moll, L., and Amanti, C. (2005). *Funds of knowledge: Theorizing practices in households, communities, and classrooms.* Mahwah, NJ: Lawrence Erlbaum.

González, N., Moll, L., Tenery, M. F., Rivera, A., Rendon, P., & Gonzáles, R. (1995). Funds of knowledge for teaching in Latino households. *Urban Education, 29,* 444–471.

González, R., & Ayala-Alcantar, C. (2008). Critical caring: Dispelling Latino stereotypes among pre-service teachers. *Journal of Latinos and Education, 7,* 129–143. DOI: 10.1080/15348430701828699.

Gordon, E., & Yowell, C. (1999). Cultural dissonance as a risk factor in the development of students. In E. Gordon (Ed.), *Education and justice: A view from the back of the bus* (pp. 34–51). New York: Teachers College Press.

Grabe, W., & Stoller, L. F. (2002). *Teaching and researching reading.* Harlow, U.K.: Pearson Education.

Green, E., Deschamps, J., & Páez, D. (2005). Variation of individualism and collectivism within and between 20 countries: A typological analysis. *Journal of Cross-Cultural Psychology, 36,* 321–339.

Greenfield, P., Quiroz, B., & Raeff, C. (2000). Cross-cultural conflict and harmony in the social construction of the child. In S. Harkness, C. Raeff, & C.M. Super (Eds.), *Variability in the social construction of the child* (pp. 93–108). New Directions in Child Development, no. 87. San Francisco: Jossey-Bass.

Gunderson, L. (2000). Voices of the teenage diasporas. *Journal of Adolescent & Adult Literacy, 43,* 692–706.

Gunning, T.G. (2008). *Creating literacy instruction for all students* (6th ed.). Boston: Allyn & Bacon.

Guthrie, J., & Wigfield, A. (2000). Engagement and motivation in reading. In M. Kamil, P. Mosenthal, P. Pearson, & R. Barr (Eds.), *Handbook of reading research volume III* (pp. 403–422). Mahwah, NJ: Lawrence Erlbaum.

Gutiérrez, K., & Rogoff, B. (2003). Cultural ways of learning: Individual traits or repertoires of practice. *Educational Researcher, 32,* 19–25.

Guzmán, Carrasco, A. (2000). Equity in education in El Salvador. *Cepal Review, 70,* 165–179.

Hall, E. (1976). *Beyond culture.* New York: Anchor.

Harger, J. (2008). The Montessori model in Puebla, Mexico: How one nonprofit is helping children. *Montessori Life, 20,* 20–25.

Heath, S.B. (1983). *Ways with words.* New York: Cambridge University Press.

Harris, J., & Katz, L. (2001). *Young investigators: The project approach in the early years.* New York: Teachers College Press.

Hawkins, M. (2004). Researching English and literacy development in schools. *Educational Researcher, 33,* 14–25.

Hofstede, G. (2001). *Culture's consequences: Comparing values, behaviors, institutions, and organizations across nations.* Thousand Oaks, CA: Sage Publications.

Hughes, M., & Greenhough, P. (2006). Boxes, bags and videotape: Enhancing home-school communication through knowledge exchange activities. *Educational Review, 58,* 471–487.

Ibarra, R. (2001). *Beyond affirmative action: Reframing the context of higher education.* Madison: University of Wisconsin Press.

Ishengoma, J. (2005). African oral traditions: Riddles among the Haya of Northwestern Tanzania. *International Review of Education, 51,* 139–153.

James, M.O. (1987). ESL reading pedagogy: Implications of schema-theoretical research. In J. Devine, P. Carrell, & D. Eskey (Eds.), *Research in reading in English as a second language* (pp. 175–188). Washington, DC: TESOL.

Jegede, O. (1994). African cultural perspectives and the teaching of science. In J. Solomon & G. Aikenhead (Eds.), *STS education: International perspectives on reform* (pp. 120–130). New York: Teachers College Press.

Joyce, B., Weil, M., & Calhoun, E. (2009). *Models of teaching* (8th ed.). Boston: Allyn & Bacon.

Kagitçibasi, C. (1994). A critical appraisal of individualism and collectivism: Toward a new formulation. In U. Kim, H. Triandis, C. Kagitçibasi, S. Choi, & G. Yoon (Eds.), *Individualism and collectivism: Theory, method, and applications* (pp. 52–65). Thousand Oaks, CA: Sage.

Kagitçibasi, C., Goksen, F., & Gulgoz, S. (2005). Functional adult literacy and empowerment of women: Impact of a functional literacy program in Turkey. *Journal of Adolescent & Adult Literacy, 44,* 458–466.

Kee, D.W., & Davies, L. (1990). Mental effort and elaborations: Effects of accessibility and instruction. *Journal of Experimental Child Psychology, 49,* 264–274.

Kim, K.H., (2005). Learning from each other: Creativity in East Asian and American education. *Creativity Research Journal, 17,* 337–347.

Kim, U. (1994). Individualism and collectivism: Conceptual clarification and elaboration. In U. Kim, H. Triandis, C. Kagitçibasi, S. Choi, & G. Yoon (Eds.), *Individualism and collectivism. Theory, method, and applications* (pp. 19–40). Thousand Oaks, CA: Sage.

Koch, J. (2007). How schools can best support Somali students and their families. *International Journal of Multicultural Education, 9,* 1–15.

Kress, G. (2003). *Literacy in the new media age.* London: Routledge Press.

Krathwohl, D. (2002). A revision of Bloom's taxonomy: An overview. *Theory into Practice, 41,* 212–264.

Kruidenier, J. (2002). *Research-based principles for adult basic education reading instruction*. Washington, DC: National Institute for Literacy.

Ladson-Billings, G. (1995). Toward a theory of culturally relevant pedagogy. *American Educational Research Journal, 32*, 465–491.

Lave, J. (1996). Teaching as learning, in practice. *Mind, Culture, and Activity, 3*, 149–164.

Lee, O. (2005). Science education with English Language Learners: A synthesis and research agenda. *Review of Educational Research, 75*, 491–530.

Levine, R.A., Dixon, S., Richman, A., Leidman, P., Keefer, C., et al. (1994). *Child care and culture: Lessons from Africa*. Cambridge, U.K.: Cambridge University Press.

Lin, X., Bransford, J., Hmelo, C., Kantor, R., Hickey, D. Secules, T., Petrosino, A., & Goldman, S. (1995). Instructional design and development of learning communities: an invitation to a dialogue. *Educational Technology, 35*, 53–63.

Lucas, T., Henze, R., & Donato, R. (1990). Promoting the success of Latino language minority students. An exploratory study of six high schools. *Harvard Educational Review, 60*, 315–341.

Lujan, J. (2008). Linguistic and cultural adaptation needs of Mexican American students related to multiple-choice tests. *Journal of Nursing Education, 47*, 327–330.

Luria, A. R. (1979). *The making of mind*. Cambridge, MA: Harvard University Press.

Lustig, M., & Koester, J. (2009). *Intercultural competence: Interpersonal communication across cultures* (6th ed.). Boston: Allyn & Bacon.

Lynch, J. (2009). Print literacy engagement of parents from low-income backgrounds: Implications for adult and family literacy programs. *Journal of Adolescent and Adult Literacy, 52*, 509–521.

Magro, K. (2008). Exploring the experiences and challenges of adults from war-affected backgrounds: New directions for literacy educators. *Adult Basic Education and Literacy Journal, 2*, 24–33.

Marshall, H. W. (1994). Hmong/English Bilingual Adult Literacy Project. Final report of research conducted under the National Institute for Literacy, grant #X257A20457. Green Bay: University of Wisconsin.

Marshall, H. W. (1998). A mutually adaptive learning paradigm (MALP) for Hmong students. *Cultural Circles, 3*, 134–149.

Marshall, H.W., & DeCapua, A. (2010). The newcomer booklet: A project for limited formally schooled students, *ELT Journal*, doi: 10.1093/elt/ccp100.

Marshall, H. W., DeCapua, A., & Antolini, C. (2010). Building literacy for SLIFE through social studies, *Educator's Voice, 3*, 56–65.

Martin, P. (2008). Educational discourses and literacy in Brunei Darusalam. *The International Journal of Bilingual Education and Bilingualism, 22*, 206–225.

Martinello, M. (2008). Language and the performance of English-language learners in math word problems. *Harvard Educational Review, 78*, 333–368.

Martinez, I. (2009). What's age gotta do with it? Understanding the age-identities and school-going practices of Mexican immigrant youth in New York City. *High School Journal, 92*, 34–48.

Marzano, R., & Kendall, J. S. (2008). *Designing and assessing educational objectives: Applying the new taxonomy*. Thousand Oaks, CA: Corwin.

McMaster, K.N., & Fuchs, D. (2002). Effects of cooperative learning on the academic achievement of students with learning disabilities: An update of Tateyama-Sniezek's review. *Learning Disabilities Research & Practice, 17*, 107–117.

Mejía-Arauz, R., Rogoff, B., Dexter, A., & Najafi, B. (2007). Cultural variation in children's social organization. *Child Development, 78*, 1001–1014.

Mendrinos, R. (1997). *Using educational technology with at-risk students: A guide for library media specialists and teachers*. Westport, CT: Greenwood Press.

Menken, K. (2008). *English learners left behind: Standardized testing as language policy.* Clevedon, U.K.: Multilingual Matters.

Mertler, C. (2009). *Action research: Teachers as researchers in the classroom* (2nd ed.). Los Angeles: Sage.

Mestre, J. (2002). *Transfer of learning: Issues and research agenda.* Arlington, VA: National Science Foundation.

Minnesota Department of Children, Families & Learning. (2002). Serving refugee students: Case studies of Somali, Bosnia, and Liberian Students in Minnesota schools. Retrieved January 27, 2010, from http://cfl.state.mn.us/mde/

Moje, E., Collazo, T., Carillo, R., & Marx R. (2001). "Maestro, What is quality?" Language, literacy, and discourse in project-based science. *Journal of Research in Science Teaching, 38,* 469–498.

Moll, L., & Greenberg, J. (1990). Creating zones of possibilities: Combining social contexts for instruction, In L. Moll (Ed.), *Vygotsky and education* (pp. 319–348). Cambridge, U.K.: Cambridge University Press.

Morrison, G. (2009). *Teaching in America* (5th ed.). Upper Saddle River, NJ: Pearson.

Morrow, L. M. (2005). *Literacy development in the early years: Helping children read and write* (5th ed.). Upper Saddle River, NJ: Pearson.

Morse, S.C. (1997). *Unschooled migrant youth: Characteristics and strategies to serve them.* Charleston, WV: Office of Educational Research and Improvement (ED). (ERIC Document Reproduction Service No. ED405158 1997-03-00). Retrieved October 10, 2009, from http://www.eric.ed.gov/ERICWebPortal/contentdelivery/servlet/ERICServlet?accno=ED405158

National Clearinghouse for English Language Acquisition. (2008). How has the English language learner (ELL) population changed in recent years? *AskNCELA.* Retrieved January 6, 2010, from www.ncela.gwu.edu/files/rcd/.../How_Has_The_Limited_English.pdf

Nattinger, J., & DeCarrico, J. (1992). *Lexical phrases and language teaching.* Oxford, U.K.: Oxford University Press.

Needham, S. (2003). "This is active learning": Theories of language, learning, and social relations in the transmission of Khmer literacy. *Anthropology & Education Quarterly, 34,* 27–49.

Nieto, S. (1994). Affirmation, solidarity, and critique: Moving beyond tolerance in multicultural education. *Multicultural Education, 1,* 9–12, 35–38.

Nieto, S. (2004). *Affirming diversity: The sociopolitical context of multicultural education* (4th ed.). New York: Allyn & Bacon.

Nieto, S. (2010). *Language, culture, and teaching: Critical perspectives* (2nd ed.) New York: Routledge.

Niyozov, S. (2008/2009, Winter). Understanding teaching beyond content and method: Insights from Central Asia. *European Education, 40,* 46–69.

Norton, B., & Toohey, K. (2004). *Critical pedagogies and language learning.* New York: Cambridge.

Nunan, D. (Ed.). (2003). *Practical English language teaching.* New York: McGraw-Hill.

Olmedo, I. (2003). Accommodation and resistance: Latinas struggle for their children's education. *Anthropology & Education, 34,* 373–395.

Ong, W. J. (1982). *Orality and literacy: The technologizing of the word.* New York: Methuen.

Oskamp, S., & Schultz, P.W. (2004). *Attitude and opinions.* Mahwah, NJ: Lawrence Erlbaum.

Oyserman, D., Coon, H., & Kemmelmeier, M. (2002). Rethinking individualism and collectivism: Evaluation of theoretical assumptions and meta-analyses. *Psychological Bulletin, 128,* 3–72.

Oyserman, D., & Lee, S. (2008). Does culture influence what and how we think? Effects of priming, individualism and collectivism. *Psychological Bulletin, 134,* 311–342.

Passel, J., & Cohn, D. (2009). *Mexican immigrants: How many come? How many leave?* Washington, DC: Pew Hispanic Center. Available at http://pewhispanic.org/publications/

Patterson, J., Hale, D., & Stessman, M. (2007/2008). Cultural contradictions and school leaving: A case study of an urban high school. *The High School Journal*, Dec./Jan., 1–15.

Peregoy, S., & Boyle, O. (2008). *Reading, writing, and learning in ESL: A resource book for teaching K-12 learners* (5th ed). New York: Pearson.

Pierce, M., & Brisk, M.E. (2002). Sharing the bilingual journey: Situational autobiography in a family literacy context. *Bilingual Research Journal, 26*, 575–597.

Pinkus, L. (Ed.). (2009). *Meaningful measurement: The role of assessments in improving high school education in the twenty-first century.* Washington, DC: Alliance for Excellent Education. Retrieved January 4, 2010, from http://www.all4ed.org/files/MeanMeasCh5Schleicher.pdf

Pridham, F. (2001). *The language of conversation.* New York: Routledge.

Richardson, K., Buran, D., Lewis, H., & López, C. (2007). Teaching science to students from rural Mexico. *Science Teacher, 74*, 36–40.

Rodriguez, N., Mira, C., Paez, N., & Myers, H. (2007). Exploring the complexities of familism and acculturation: Central constructs for people of Mexican origin. *American Journal of Community Psychology, 39*, 61–77.

Rogoff, B. (2003). The cultural nature of human development. New York: Oxford University Press.

Rong, X.L., & Shi, T. (2001). Inequality in Chinese education. *Journal of Contemporary China, 10*, 107–124.

Rothstein-Fisch, C., Trumbull, E., Isaac, A., Daley, C., & Pérez, A. (2003). When "helping someone else" is the right answer: Bridging cultures in assessment. *Journal of Latinos and Education, 2*, 123–140.

Salomon, F., & Apaza, E. (2006). Vernacular literacy on the Lake Titicaca High Plains, Peru. *Reading Research Quarterly, 41*, 304–326.

Samovar, L., & Porter, R. (2008). Intercultural communication: A reader (8th ed.). Belmont, CA: Wadsworth.

Sarroub, L., Pernicek, T., & Sweeney, T. (2007). "I was bitten by a scorpion": Reading in and out of school in a refugee's life. *Journal of Adult Literacy, 50*, 668–679.

Saxe, G.B. (1998). Candy selling and math learning. *Educational Researcher, 17*, 14–21.

Schleppegrell, M. (2004). *The language of schooling: A functional linguistics perspective.* Mahwah, NJ: Lawrence Erlbaum.

Schlosser, L. (1992). Teacher distance and student disengagement: School lives on the margin. *Journal of Teacher Education, 43*, 128–140.

Scribner, S., & Cole, M. (1981). *The psychology of literacy.* Cambridge, MA: Harvard University Press.

Short, D. (2002). Language learning in sheltered social studies classes. *TESOL Journal, 11*, 18–24.

Shuter, R. (1985). The Hmong of Laos: Orality, communication, and acculturation. In L. Samovar & R. Porter (Eds.), *Intercultural communication: A reader* (4th ed.) (pp. 102–109). Belmont, CA: Wadsworth.

Siegel, C. (2005). Implementing a research-based model of cooperative learning. *The Journal of Educational Research, 98*, 339–348.

Siegler, R., & Alibali, M. W. (2004). *Children's thinking* (4th ed.). Upper Saddle River, NJ: Pearson Prentice Hall.

Snow, C., Cancini, H., González, P., & Shriberg, E. (1989). Giving formal definitions: An oral language correlate of school literacy. In D. Bloome (Ed.), *Classrooms and literacy* (pp. 233–249). Norwood, NJ: Ablex.

Solano-Flores, G., & Trumball, E. (2003.) Examining language in context: The need for new research paradigms in the testing of English-language learners. *Educational Researcher, 32*, 3–13.

Spring, J. (2008). The intersection of cultures (4th ed.). New York: Routledge.

Street, B.B. (2007). *Literacy: An advanced resource book for students.* New York: Routledge.

Suárez-Orozco, C., Suárez-Orozco, M., & Todorova, I. (2008). *Learning a new land: Immigrant students in American society.* Cambridge, MA: Belknap.

Tomlinson, C. (1999). *The differentiated classroom: Responding to the needs of all learners.* Englewood Cliffs, NJ: Prentice-Hall.

Ting-Toomey, S., & Chung, L.C. (2005). *Understanding intercultural communication.* Los Angeles: Roxbury Publishing Company.

Toth, J. F., Jr., & Xu, X. (1999). Ethnic and cultural diversity in fathers' involvement: A racial/ethnic comparison of African American, Hispanic, and White fathers. *Youth and Society, 31,* 76–77.

Townsend, J., & Fu, D. (2001). Paw's story: A Laotian refugee's lonely entry into American literacy. *Journal of Adolescent and Adult Literacy, 45,* 104–114.

Triandis, H. (1994). *Culture and social behavior.* New York: McGraw Hill.

Triandis, H. (1995). *Individualism & collectivism.* Boulder, CO: Westview Press.

Triandis, H. (2000). Culture and conflict. *International Journal of Psychology, 35,* 145–152.

Trumbull, E., Rothstein-Fisch, C., Greenfield, P., & Quiroz, B. (2001). *Bridging cultures between home and school: A guide for teachers.* San Francisco: WestEd.

Tyler, K., Uqdah, A., Dillihunt, M., Beatty-Hazelbaker, R., Conner, T., Gadon, N., Henchy, A., Hughes, T., Mulder, S., Owens, E., Roan-Belle, C., Smith, L., & Stevens, R. (2008). Cultural discontinuity: Toward a quantitative investigation of a major hypothesis in education. *Educational Researcher, 37,* 280–297.

U.S. Department of Education. (2007). Guidance on regulations regarding assessment and accountability for recently arrived and former limited English proficient (LEP) students. Washington, DC: U.S. Department of Education. http://www2.ed.gov/policy/e/sec/guid/lepguidance.doc

Van den Branden, K., & Verhelst, M. (Eds.) (2007). *Tasks in action: Task-based language education from a classroom-based perspective.* Newcastle, U.K.: Cambridge Scholars Publishing.

Ventura, P., Pattamadilok, C., Fernandes, T., Klein, O., Morais, J., & Kolinsky, R. (2008). Schooling in Western culture promotes context-free processing. *Journal of Experimental Child Psychology, 100,* 79–88.

Villegas, A.M., & Lucas, T. (2002). *Educating culturally responsive teachers: A coherent approach.* Albany: State University of New York Press.

Vygotsky, L. (1962). *Thought and language.* Cambridge, MA: MIT Press.

Vygotsky, L. (1978). *Mind in society: The development of higher psychological processes.* M. Cole, V. John-Steiner, S. Scribner, & E. Souberman (Eds. & Trans.). Cambridge, MA: Harvard University Press. (Original work published 1934).

Walsh, C. (1999). *Enabling academic success for secondary students with limited formal schooling: A study of the Haitian literacy program at Hyde Park High School in Boston.* Providence, RI: LAB. Retrieved April 16, 2009, from http://www.alliance.brown.edu/pubs/HaitianLit.pdf

Whitescarver, K., & Kalman, J. (2009). Extending traditional explanations of illiteracy: Historical and cross-cultural perspectives. *Compare, 39,* 501–515.

Willingham, D. (2007). Critical thinking: Why is it so hard to teach? *American Educator, Summer,* 8–19.

Willingham, D. (2009). *Why don't students like school?* San Francisco: Jossey-Bass.

Wood, D. (2002). Formulaic language in acquisition and production: Implications for teaching. *TESL Canada, 20,* 1–15.

Wurzel, J. (2005). *Building community in the classroom: An intercultural approach.* Newton, MA: Intercultural Resource Corporation.

Index

Pages numbers followed by f indicates figure; t indicates table